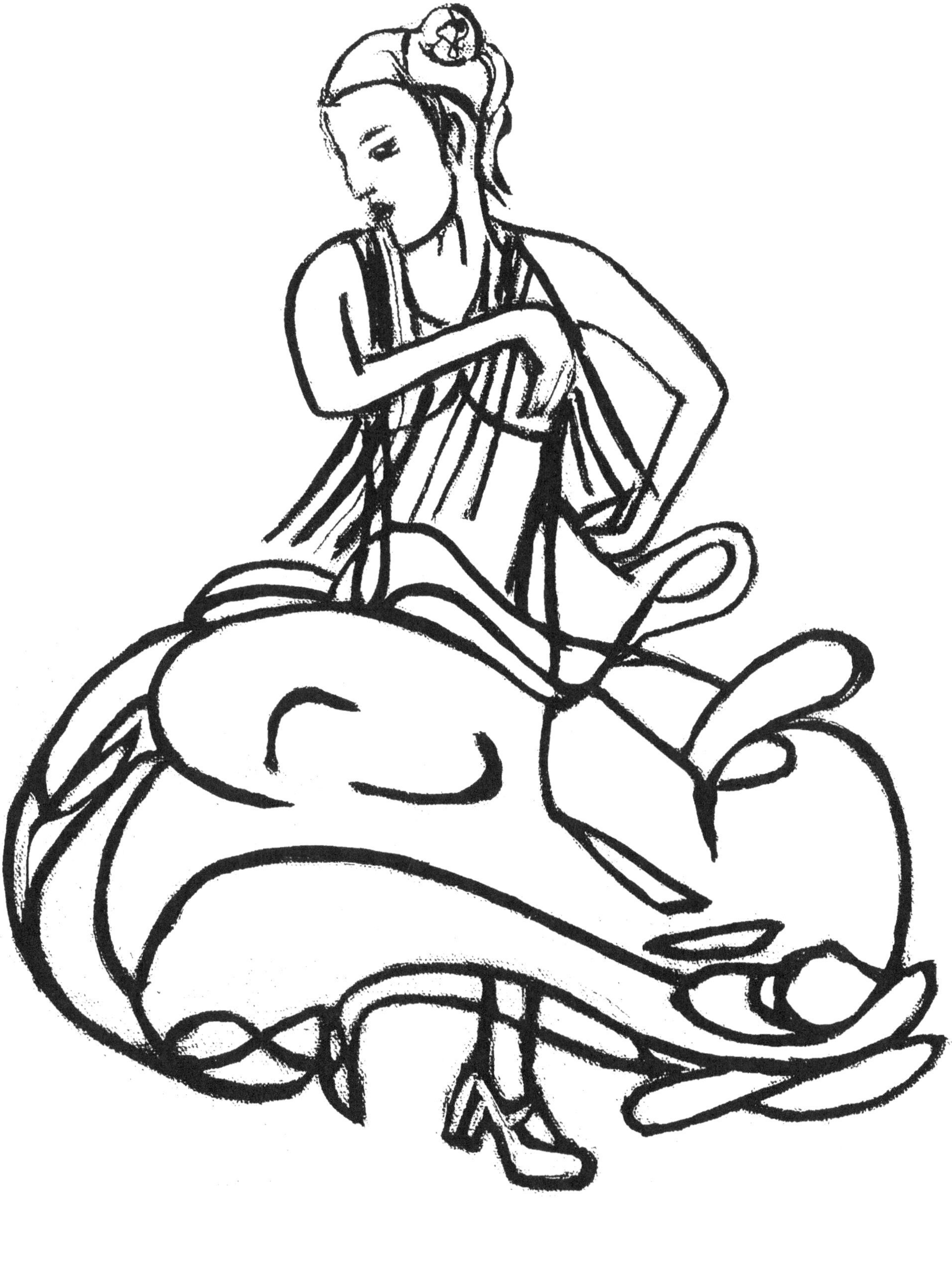

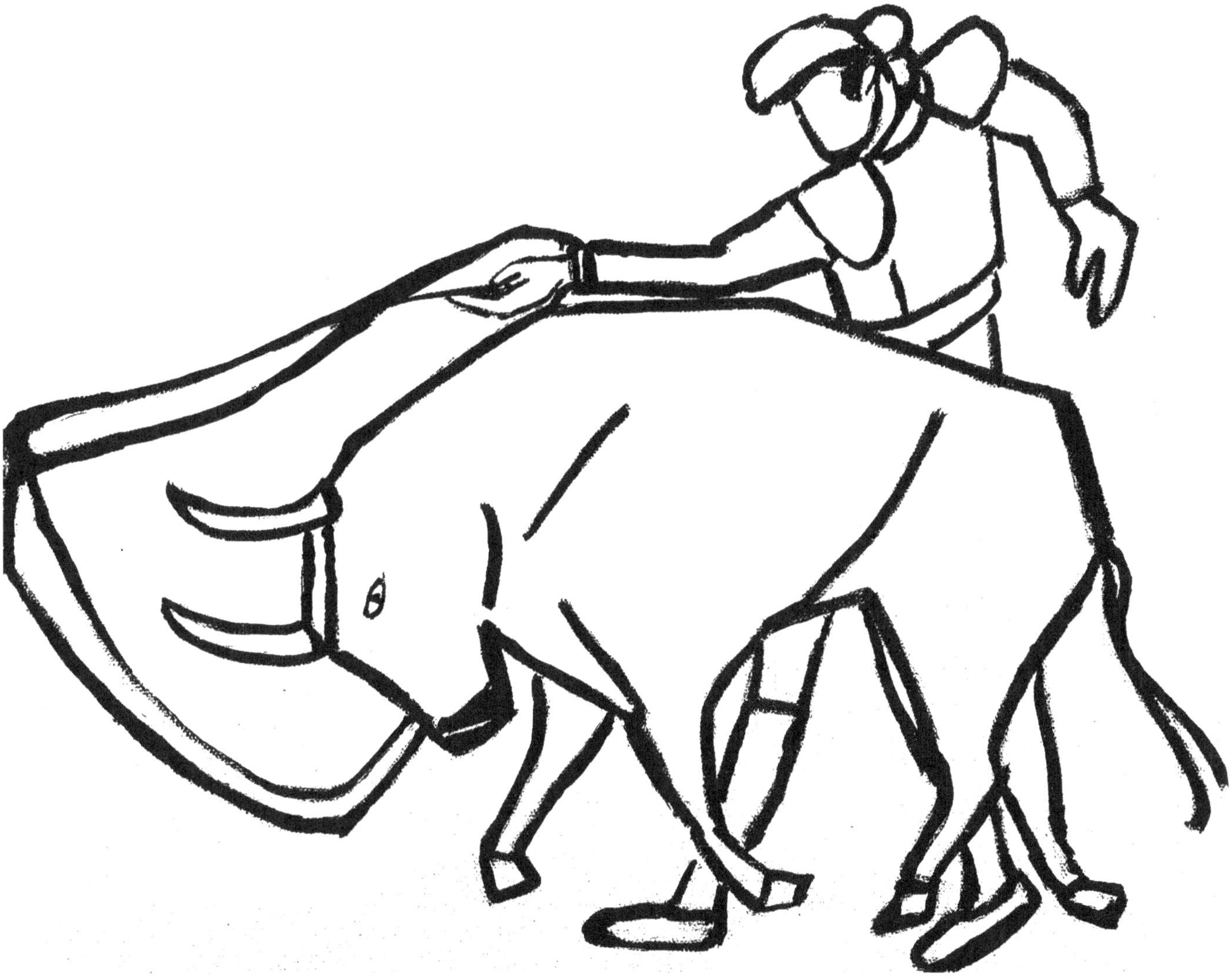

Cut Here

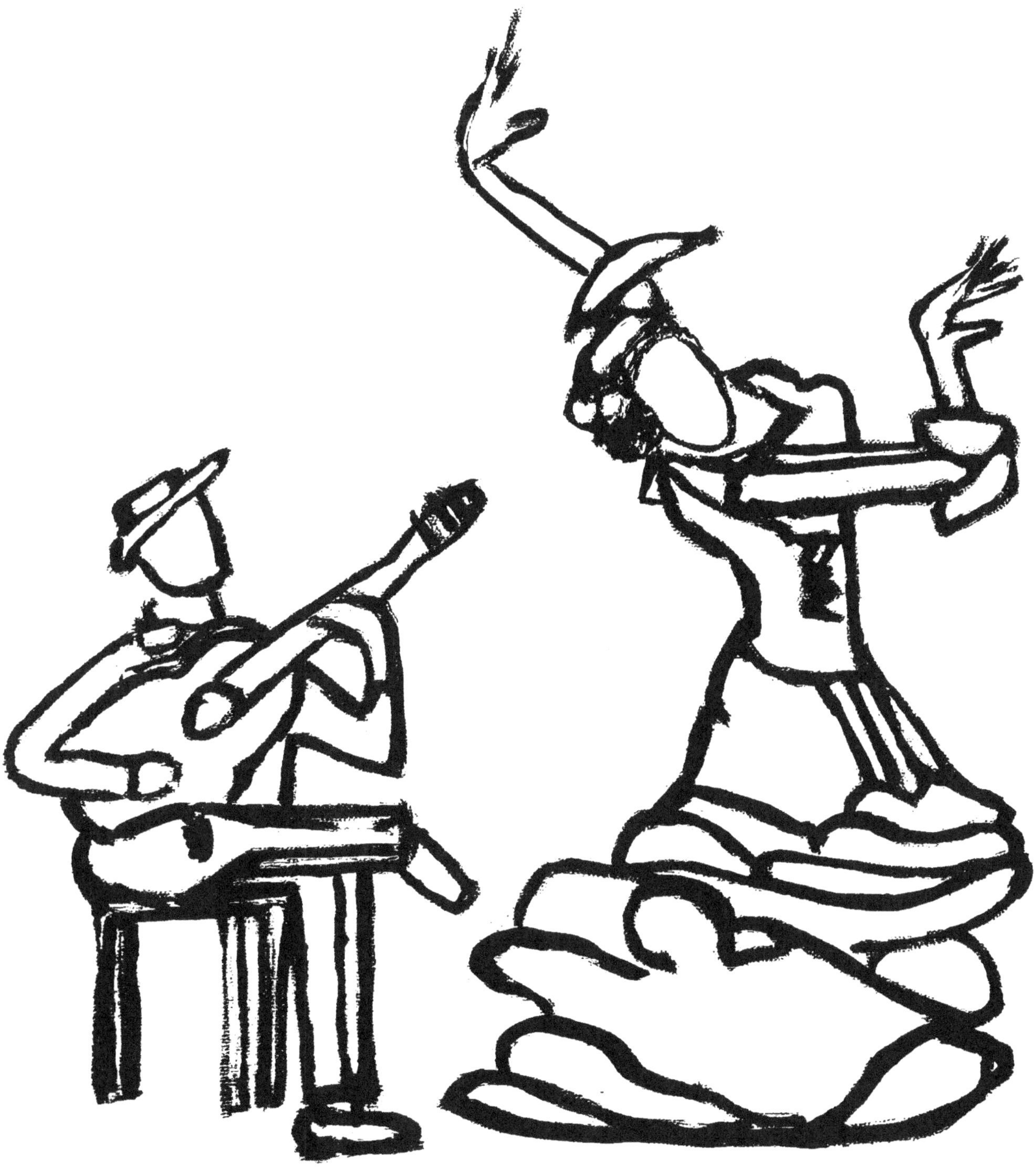

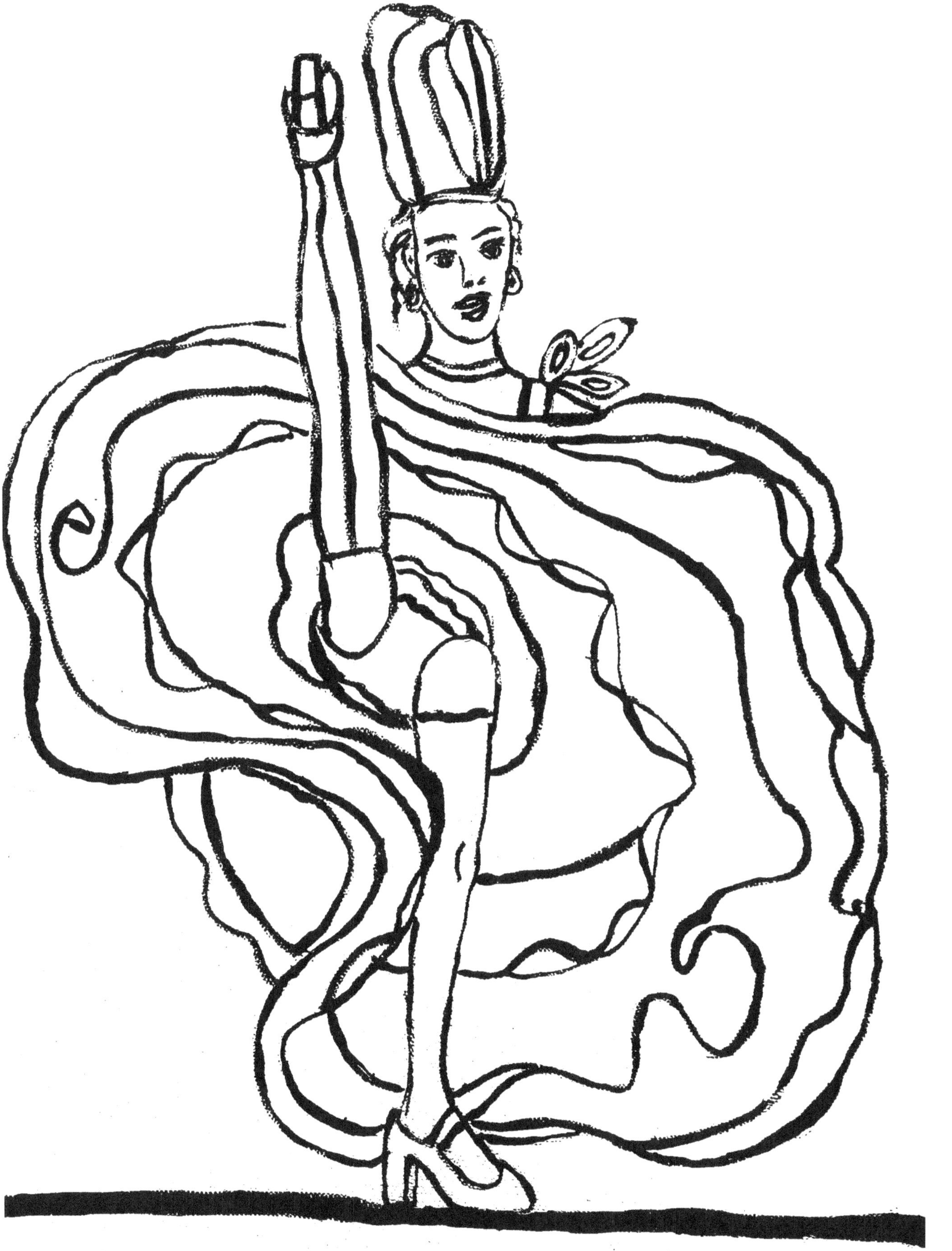

Cut Here

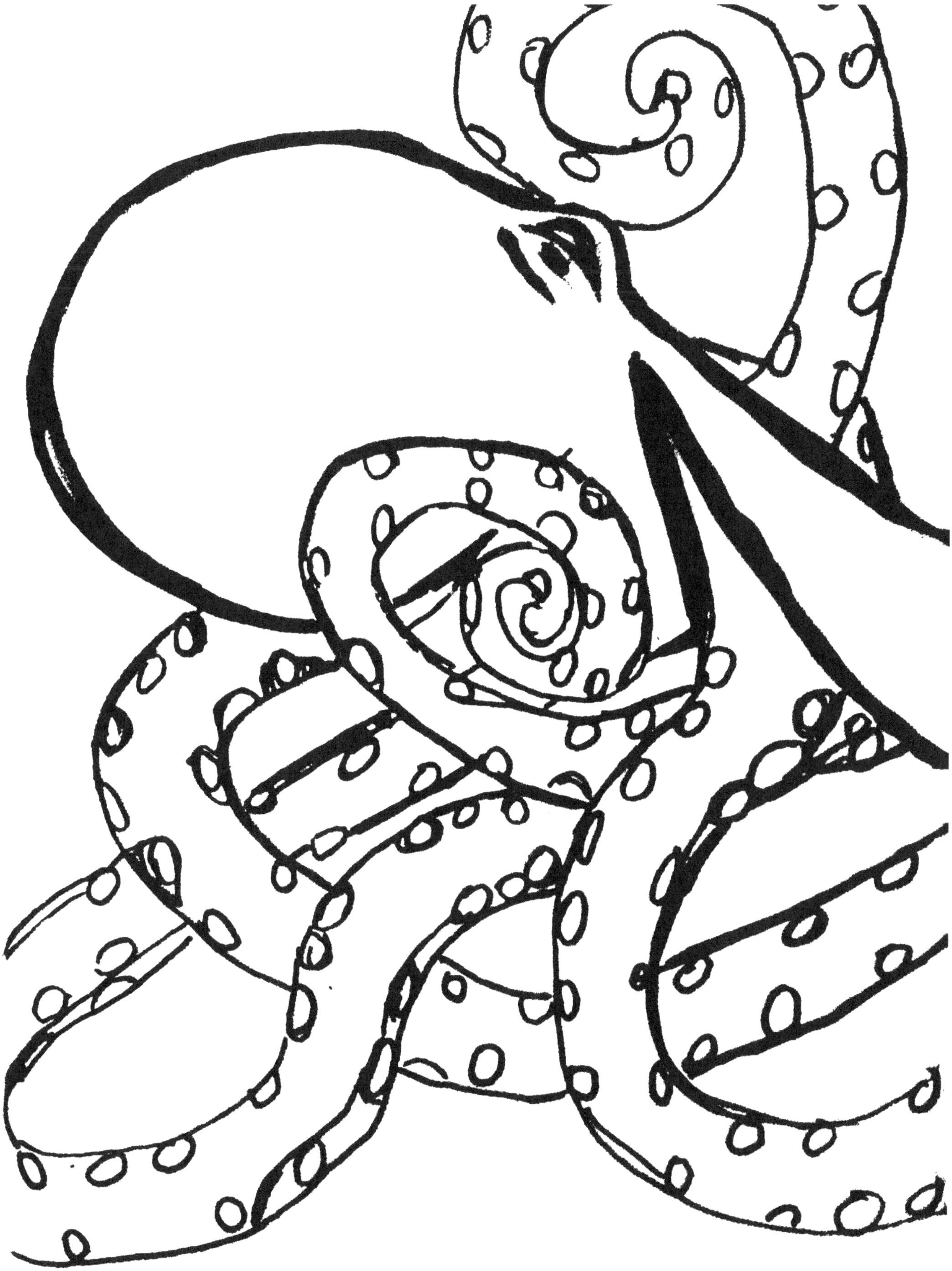

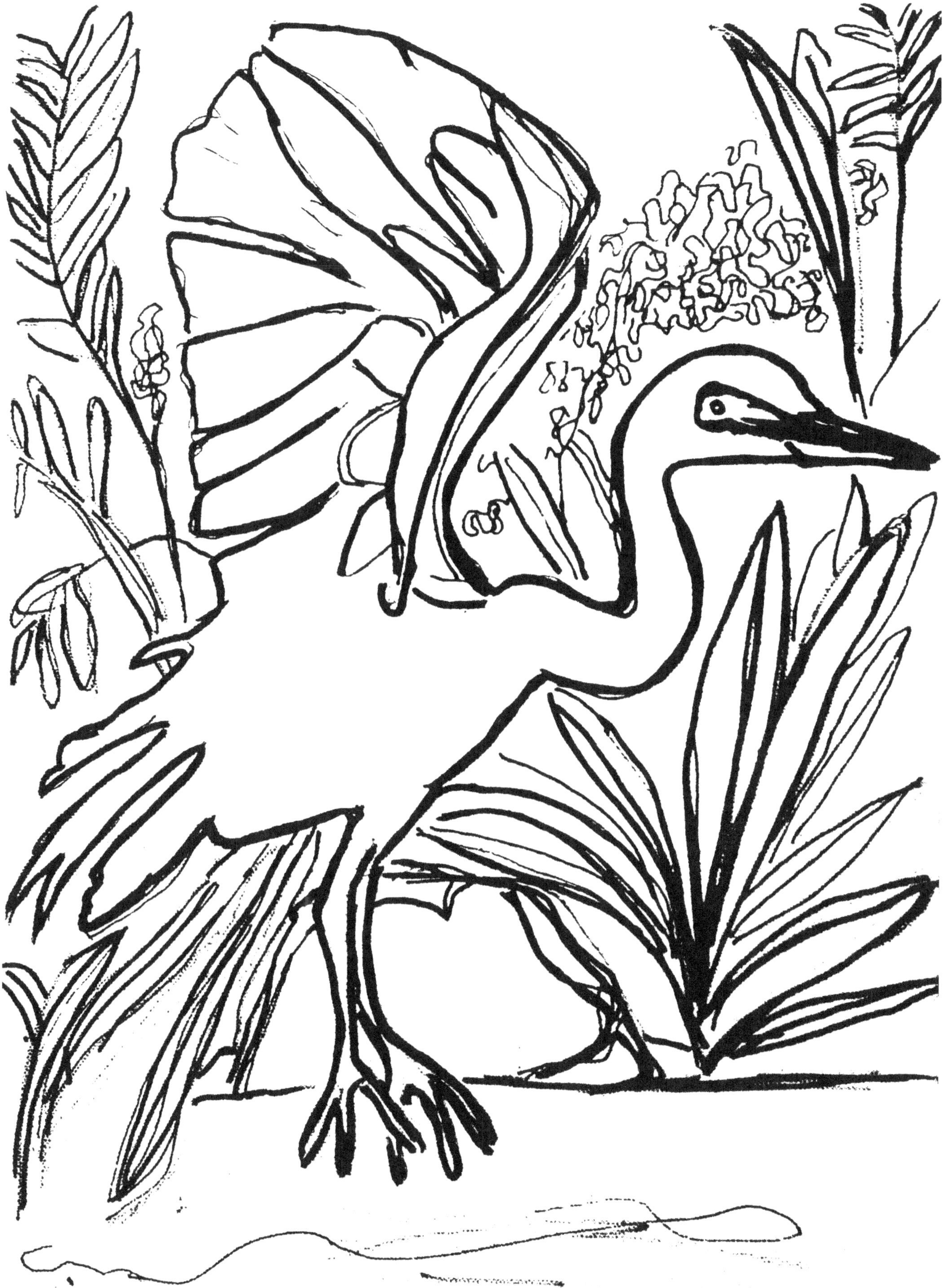

Cut Here

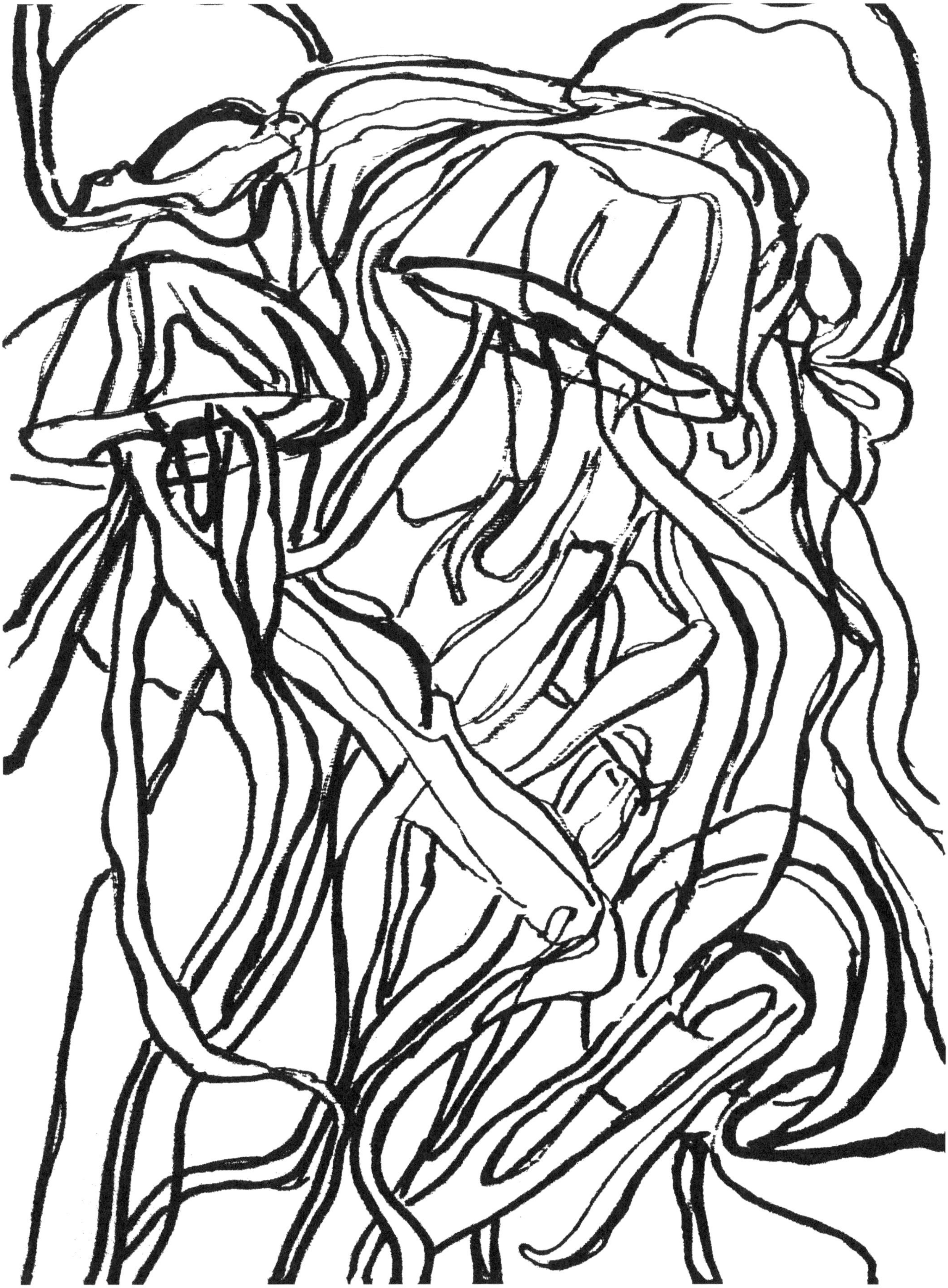

Cut Here

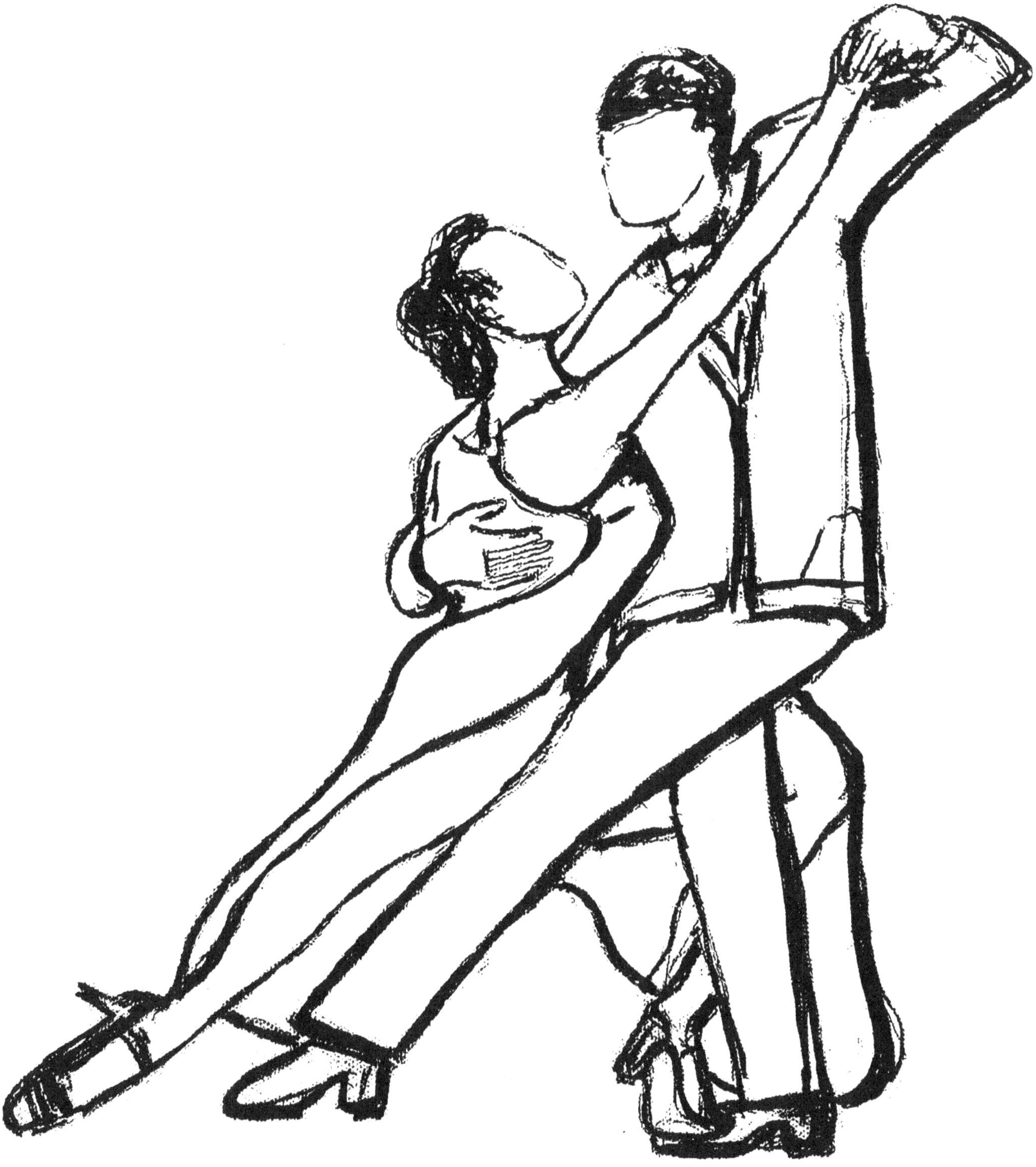

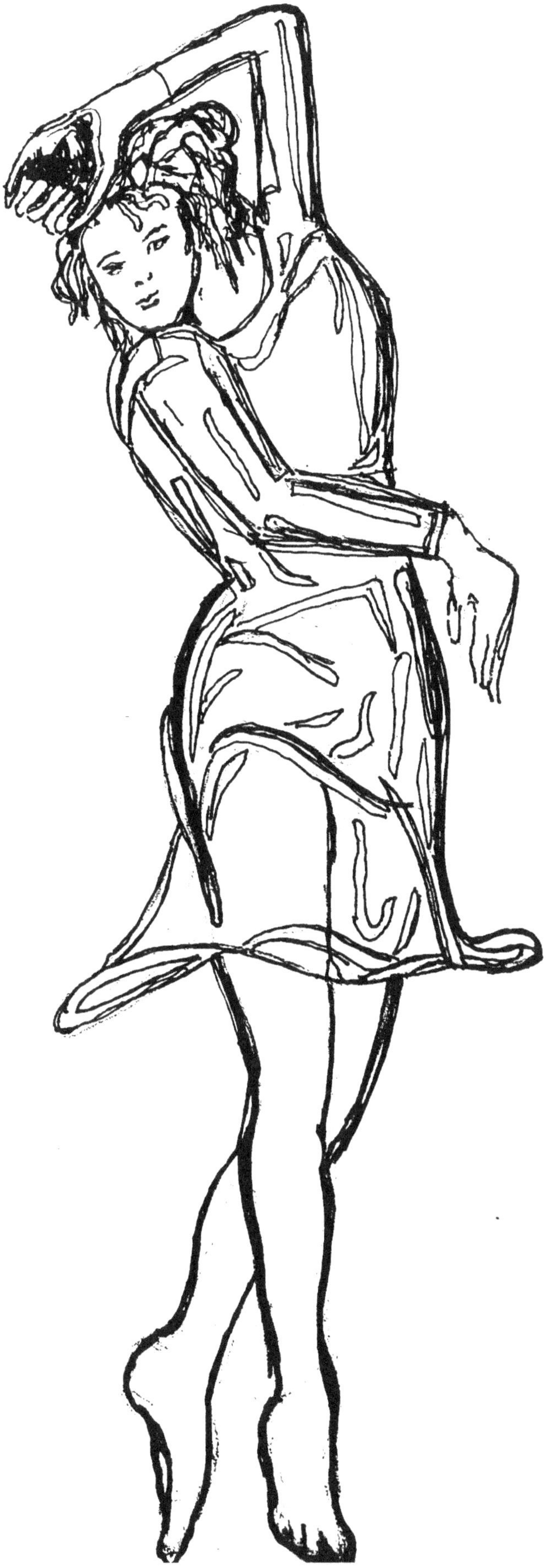

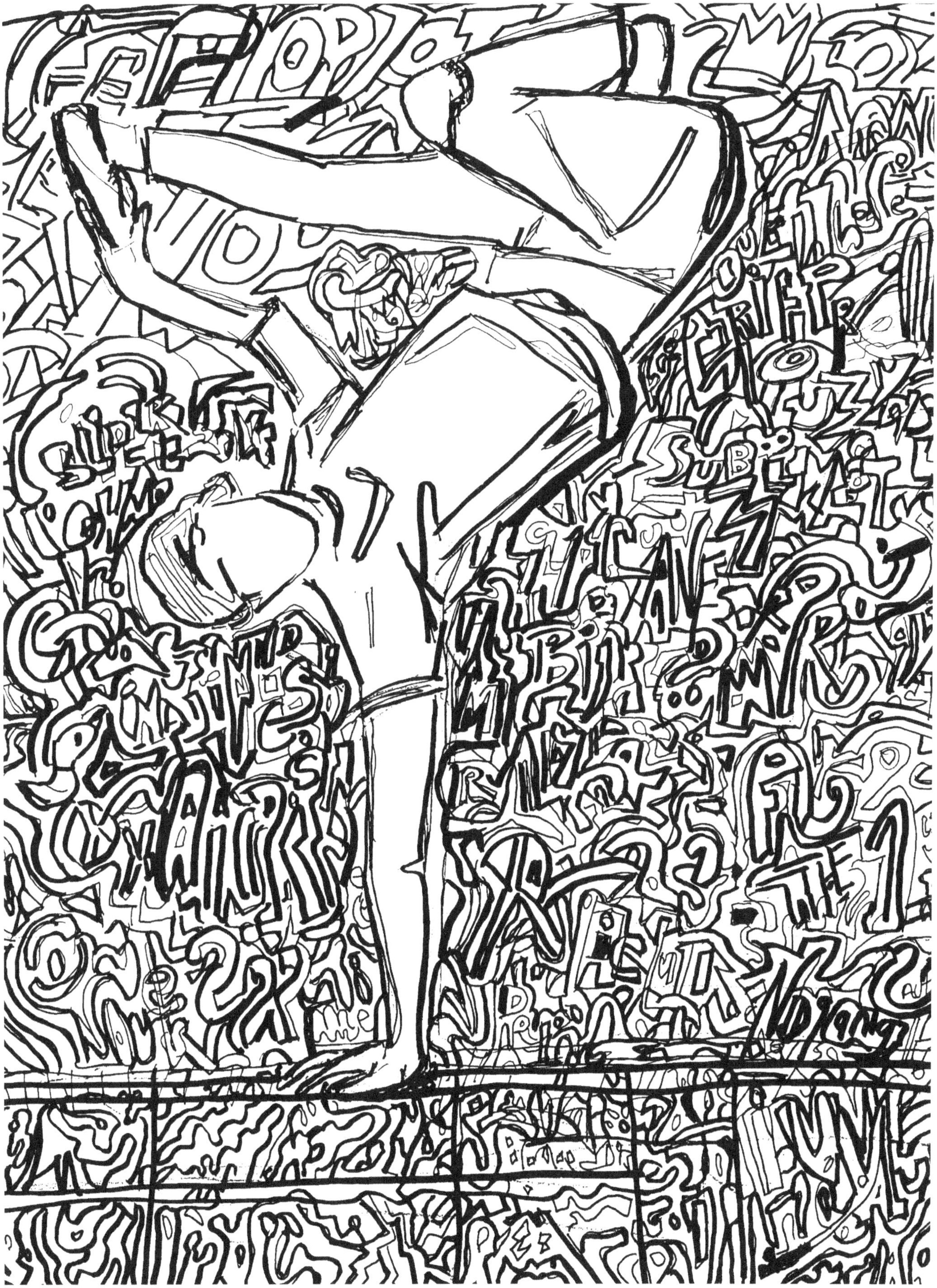

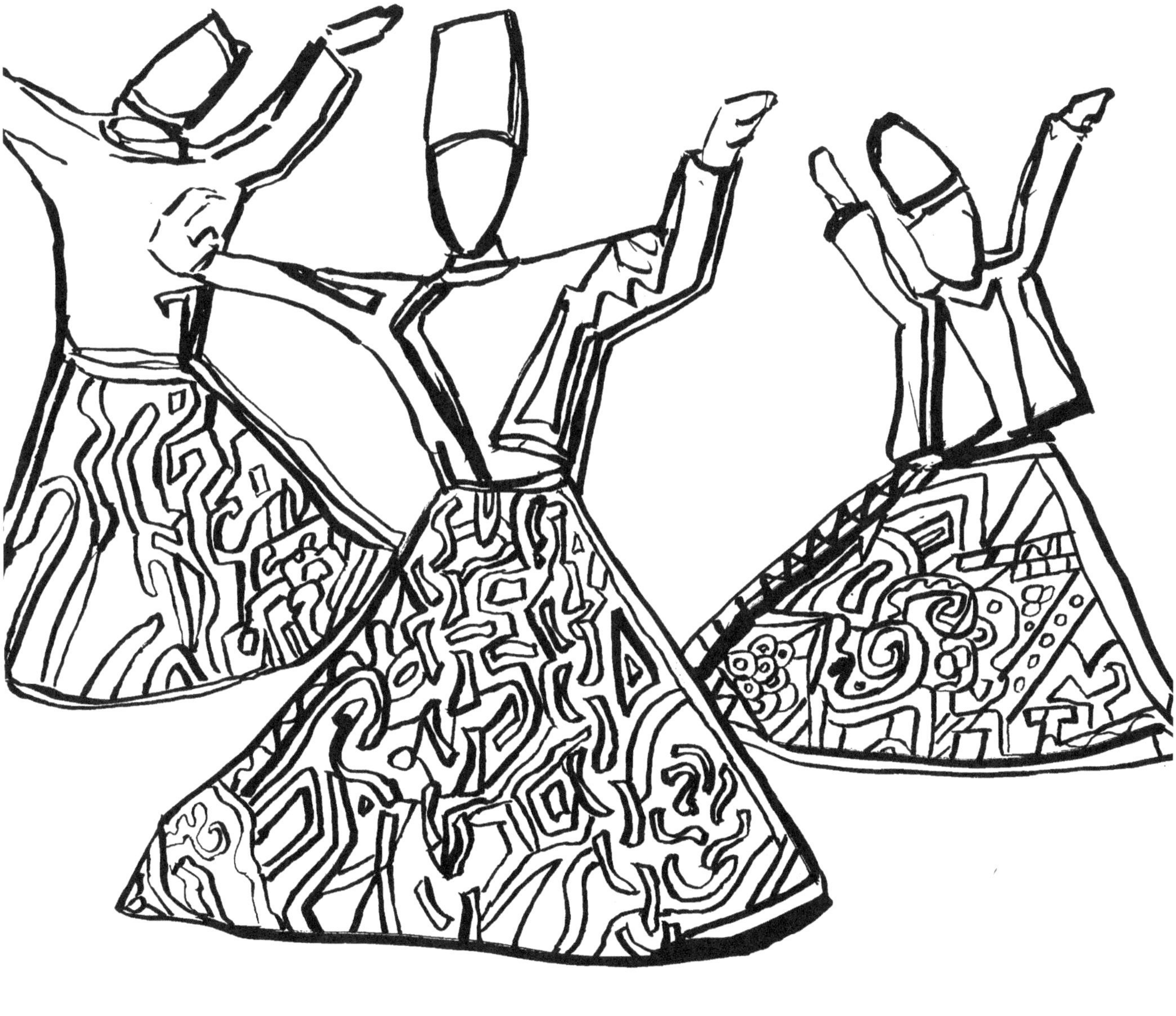

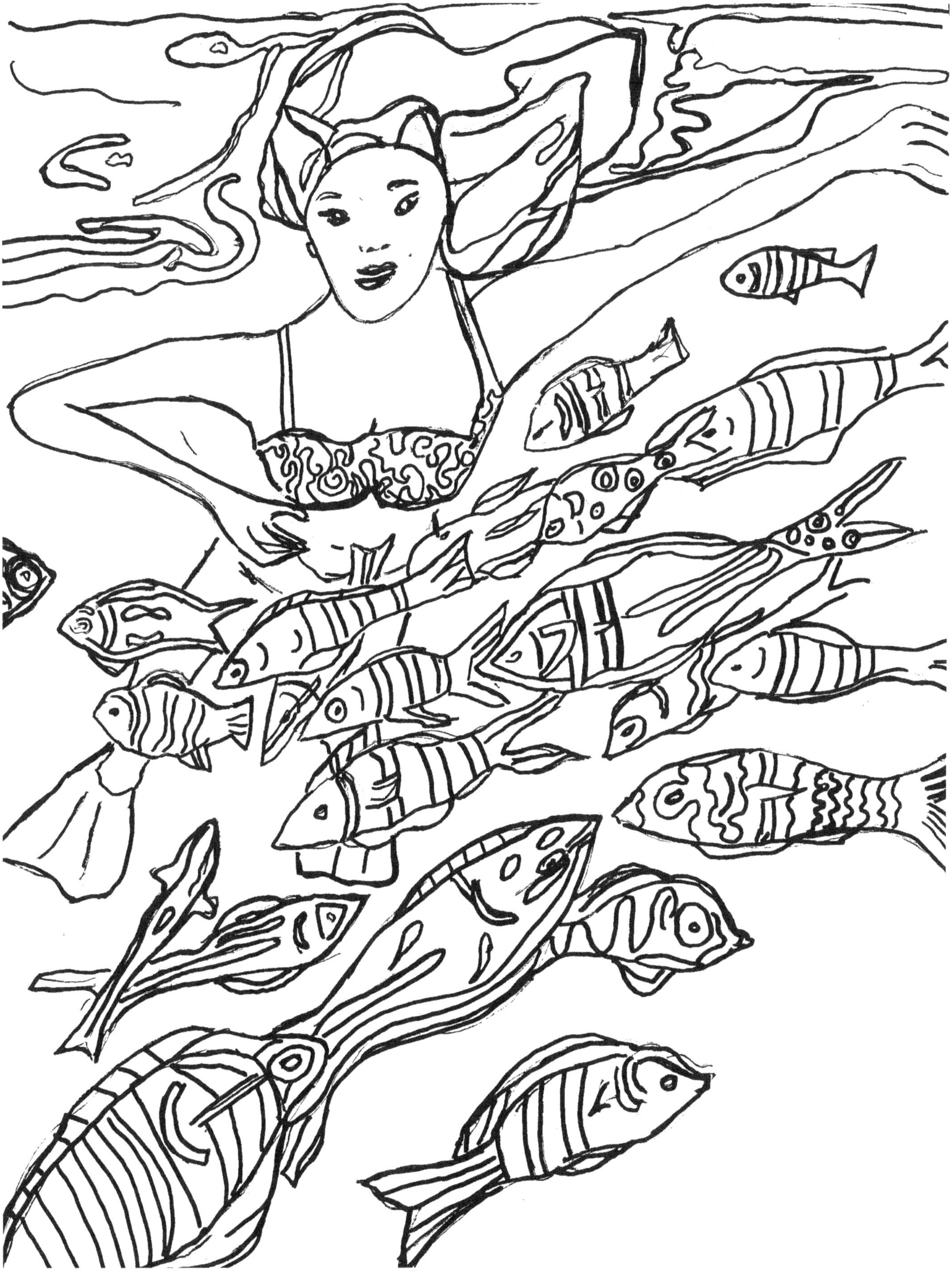

Cut Here

Cut Here

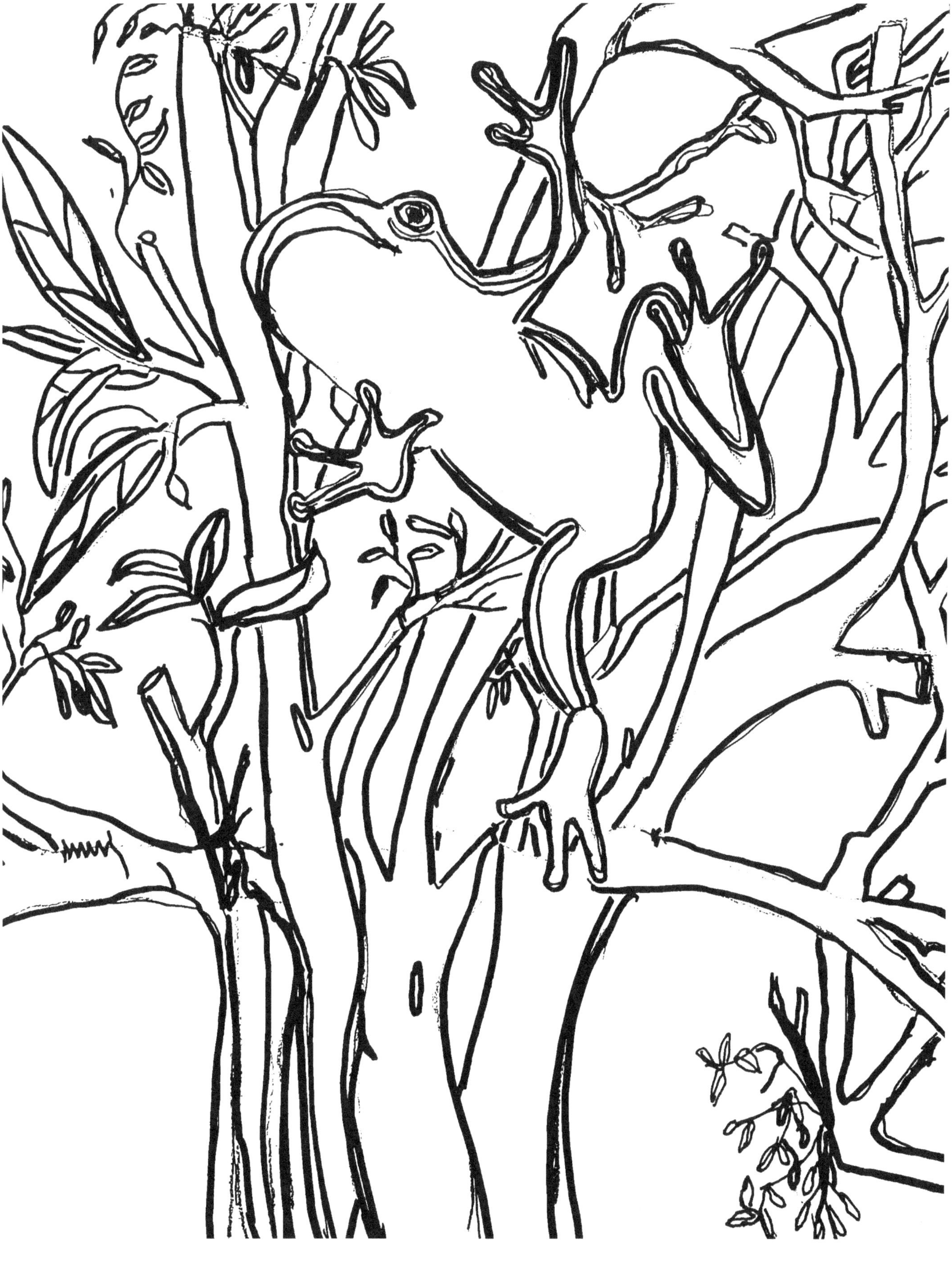

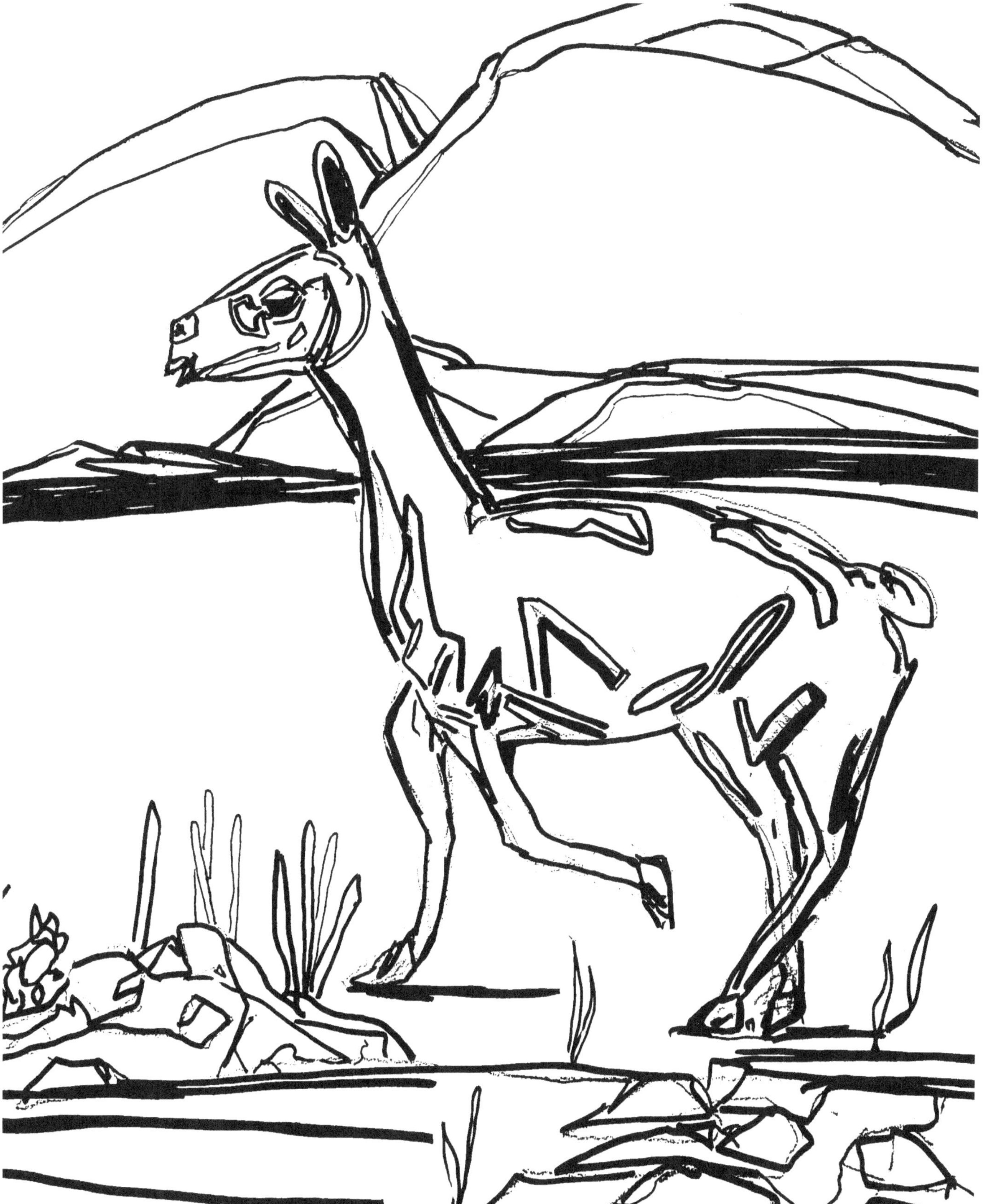

Cut Here

Cut Here

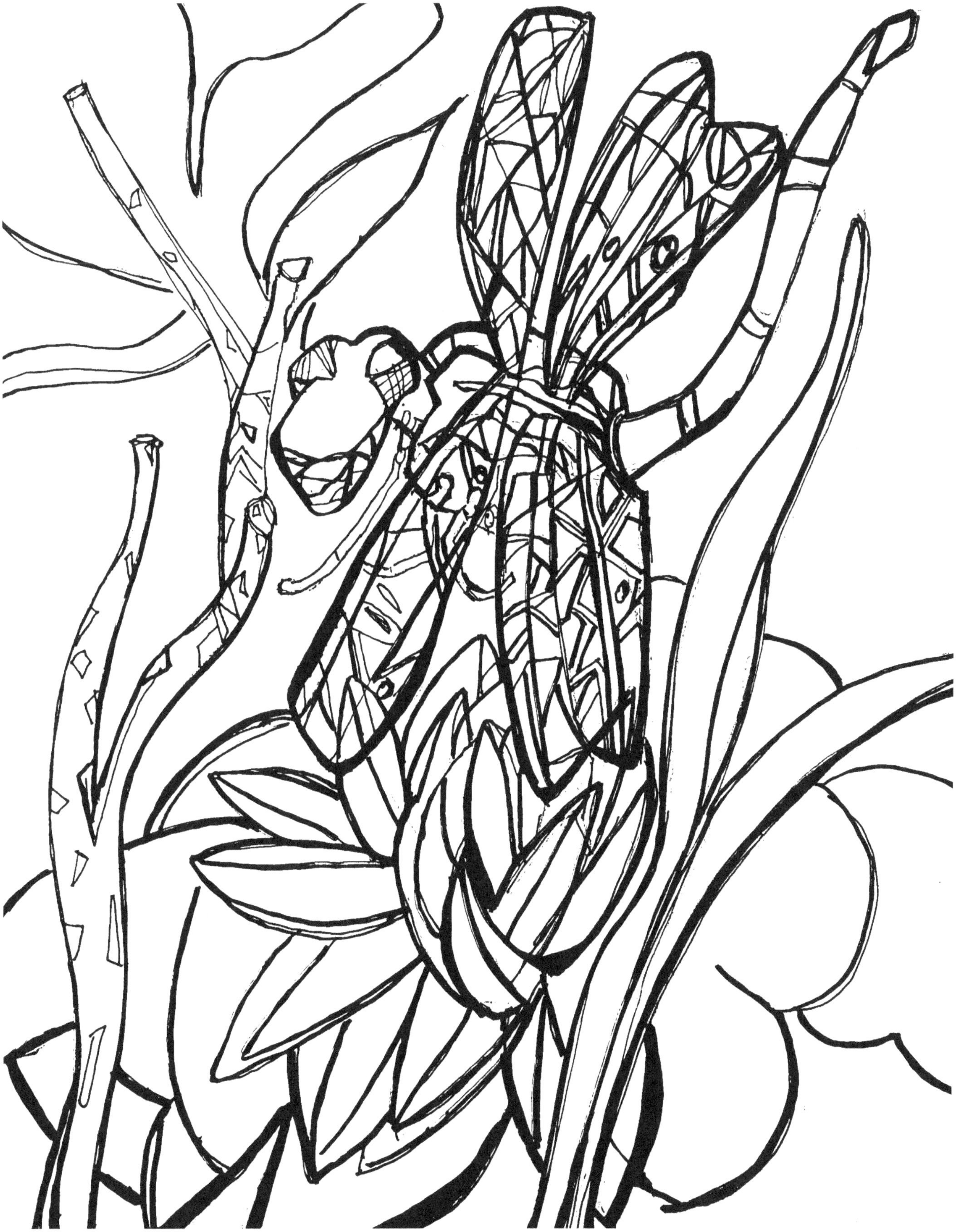

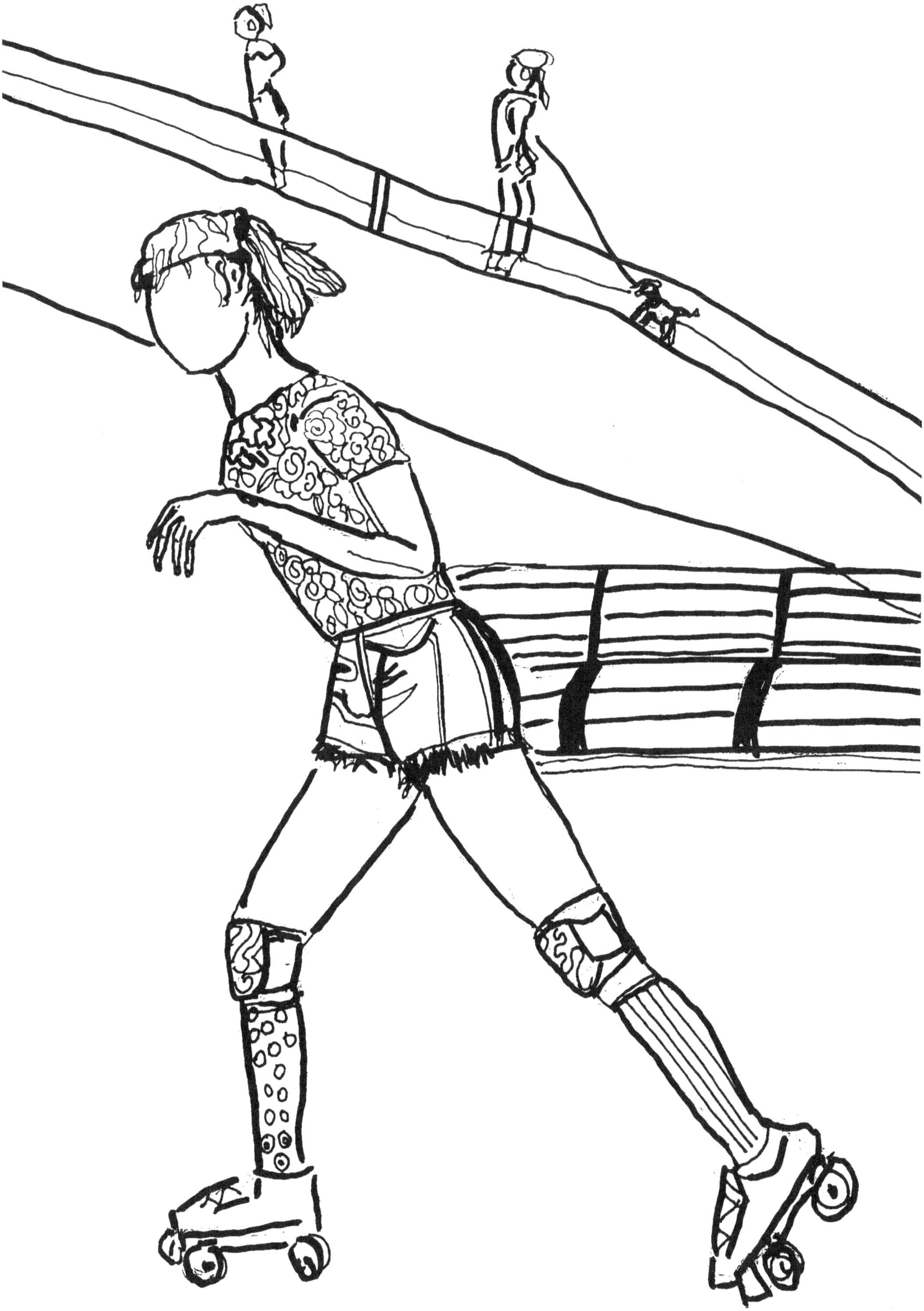

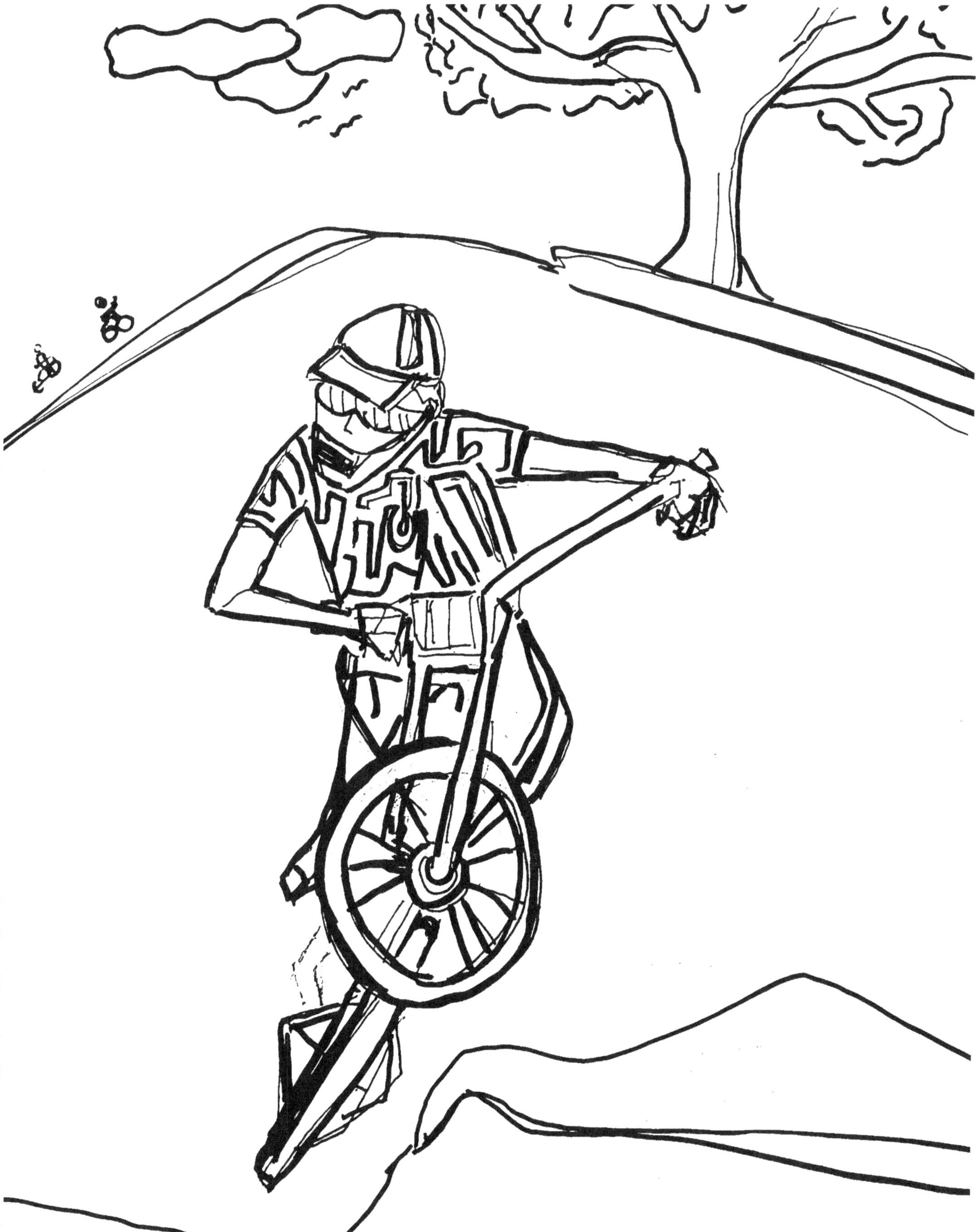

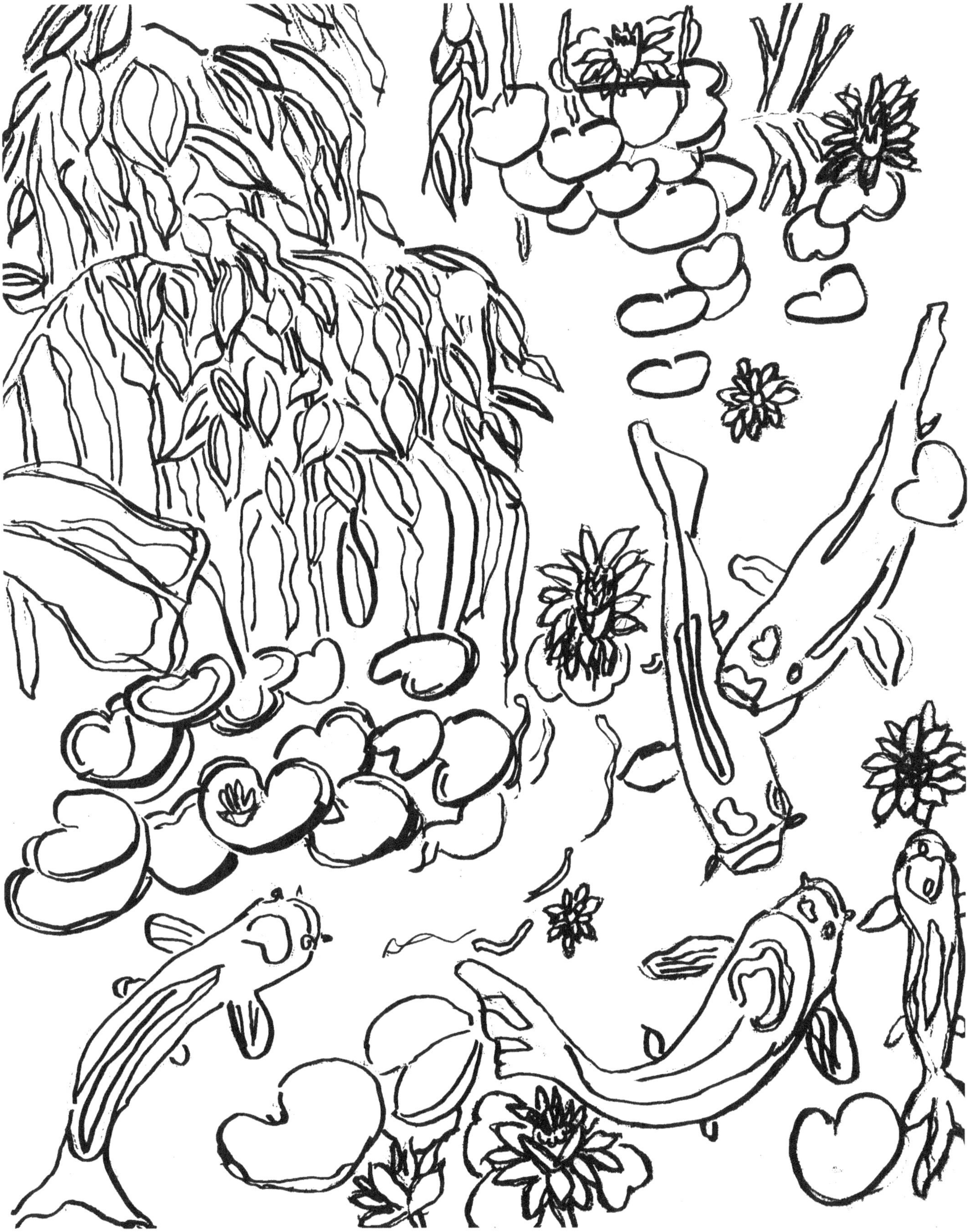

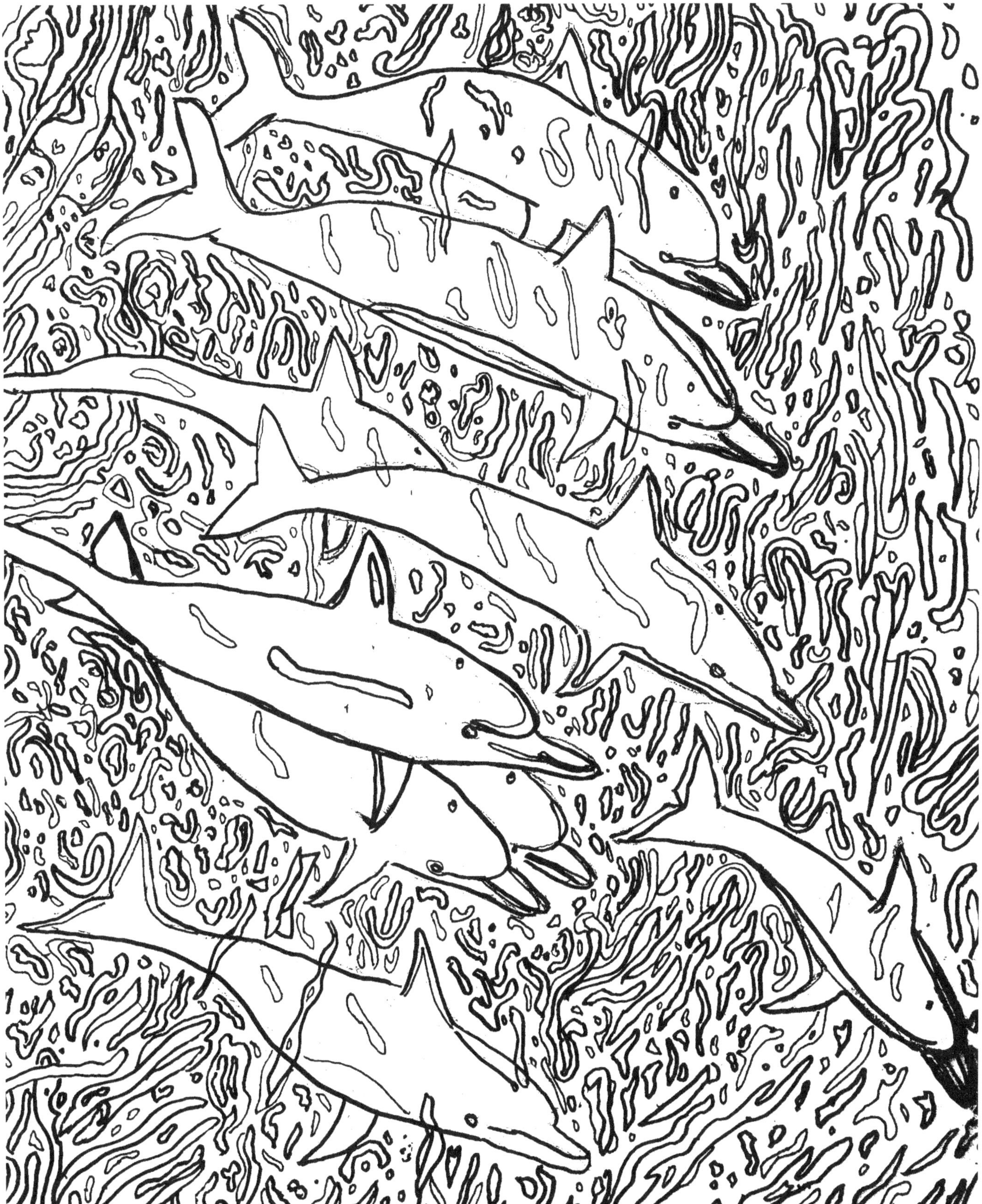

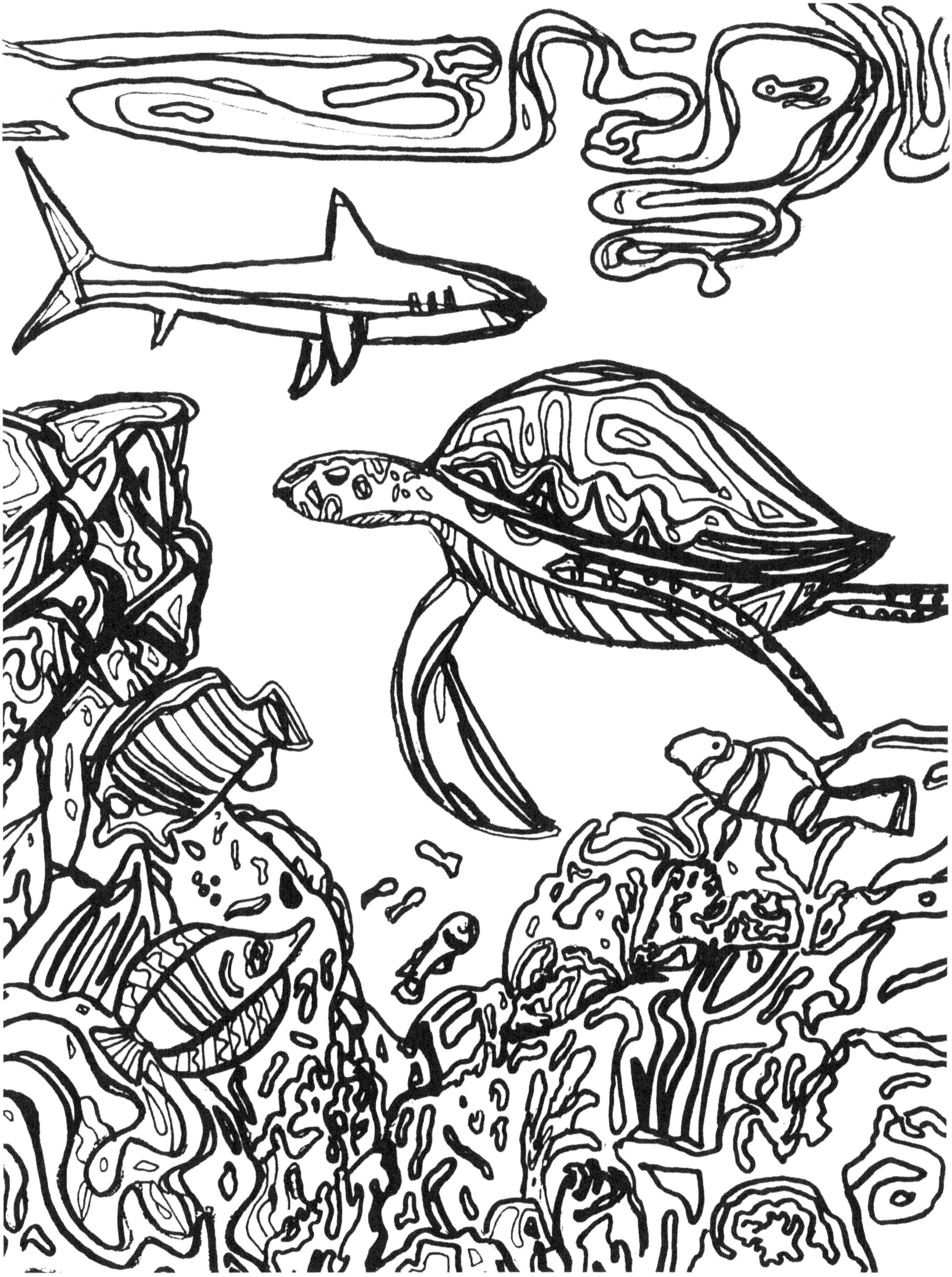

Cut Here

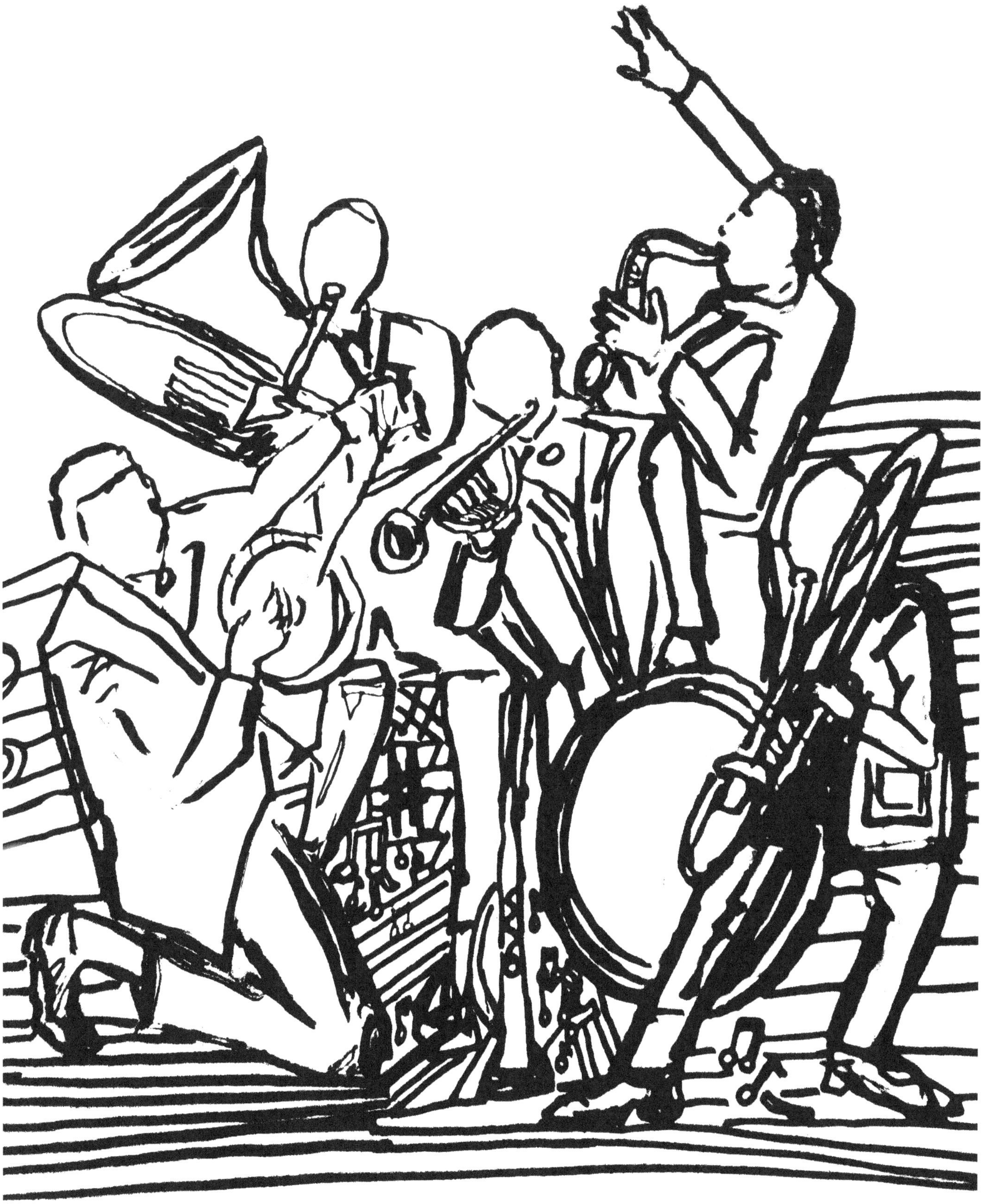

Cut Here

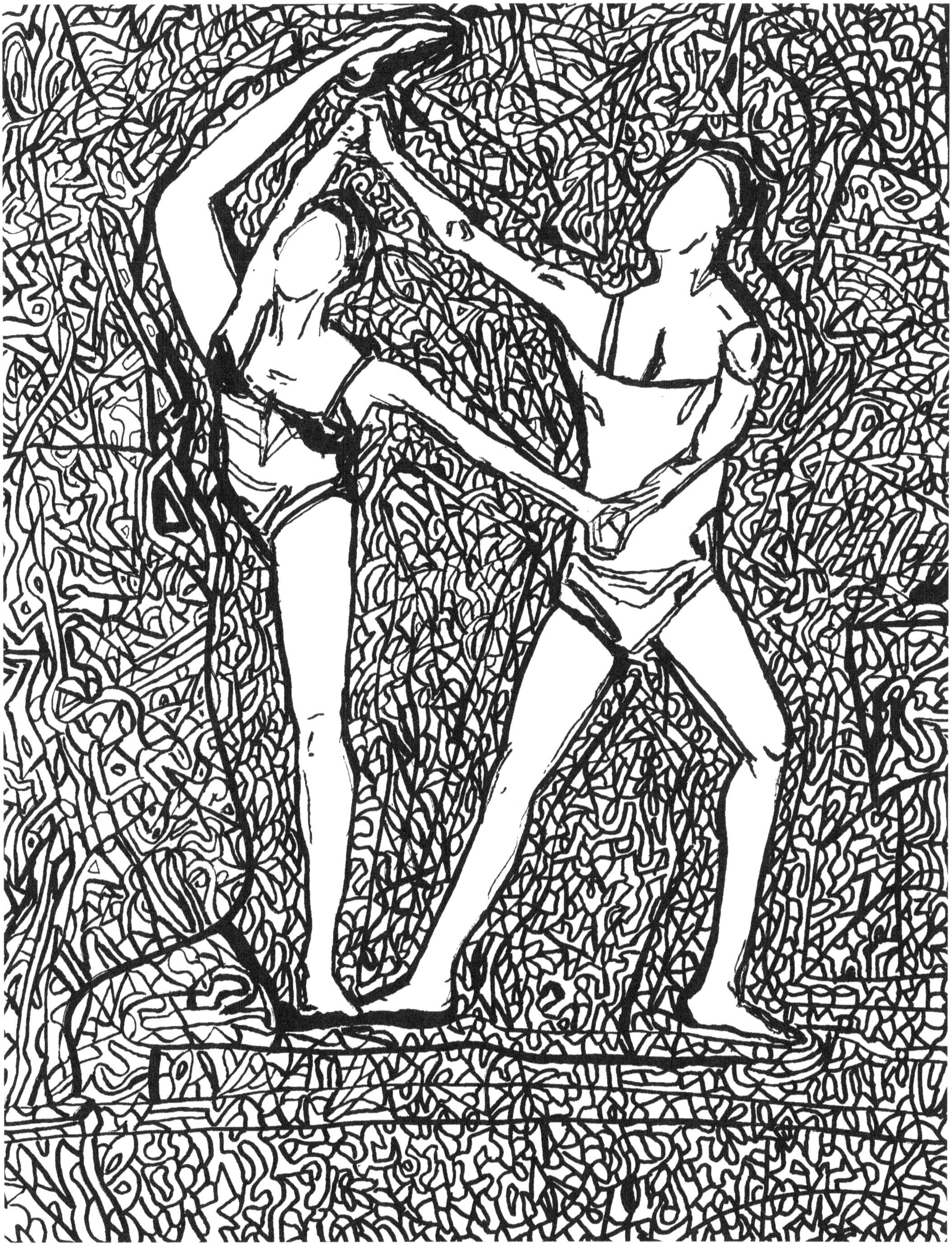

Cut Here

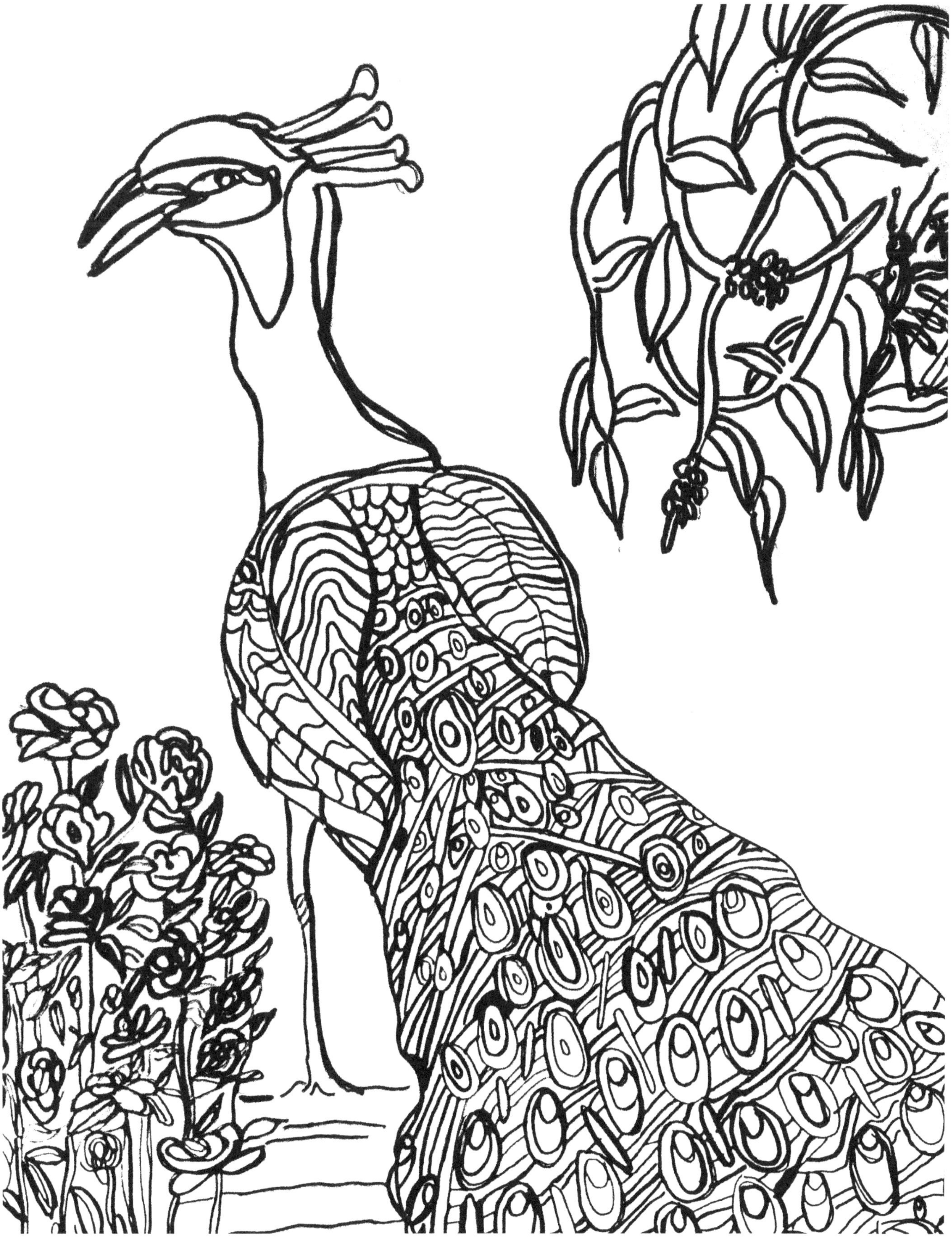

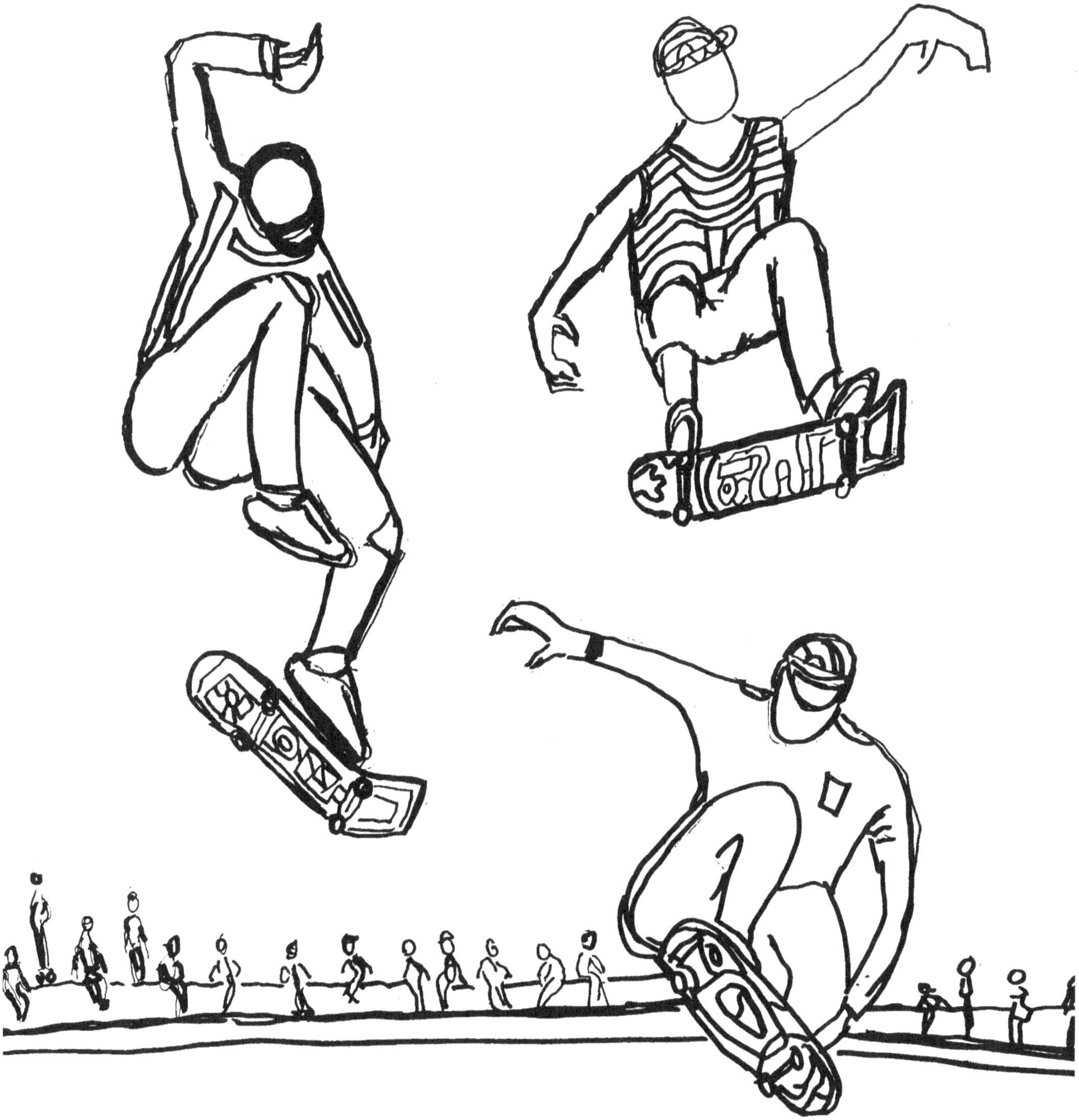

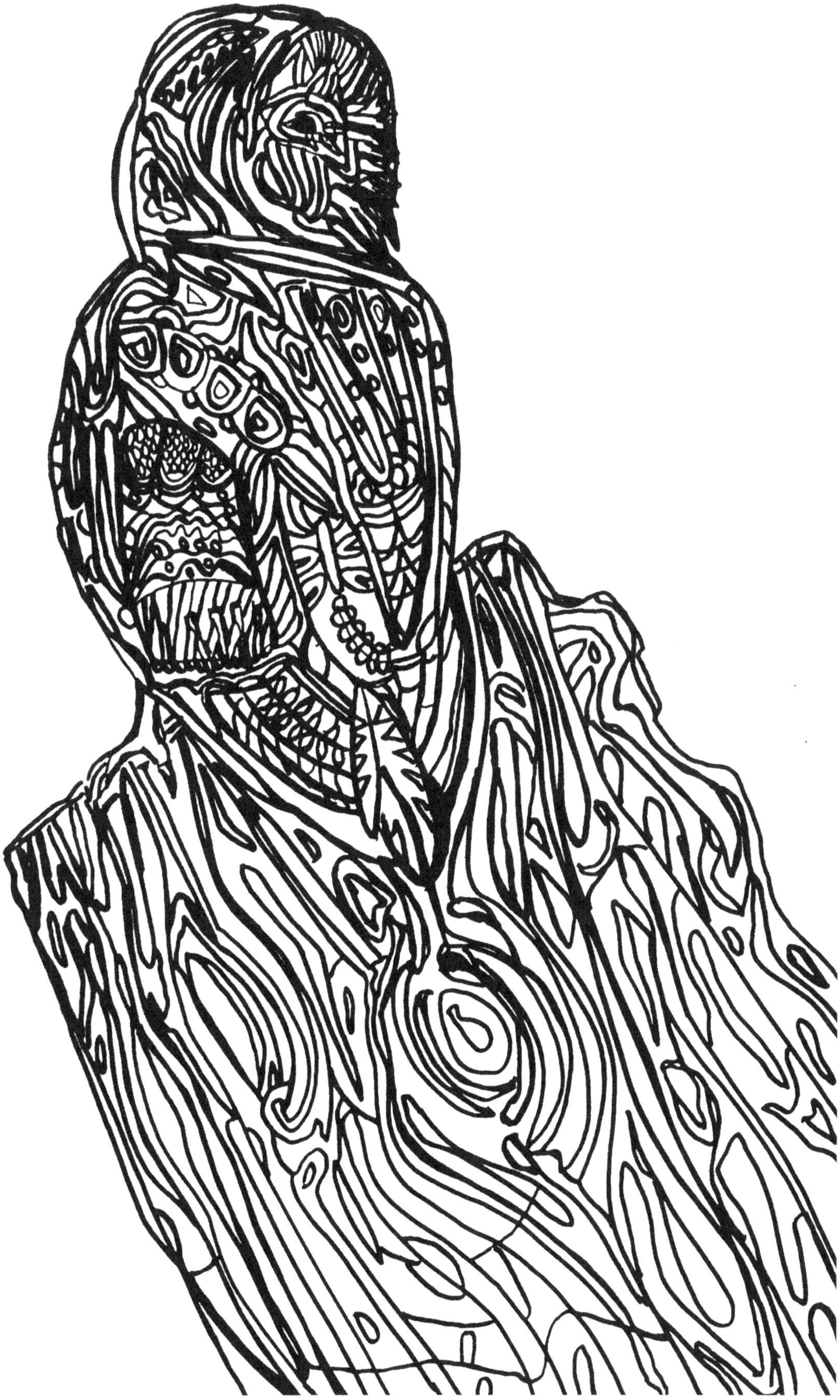

Cut Here

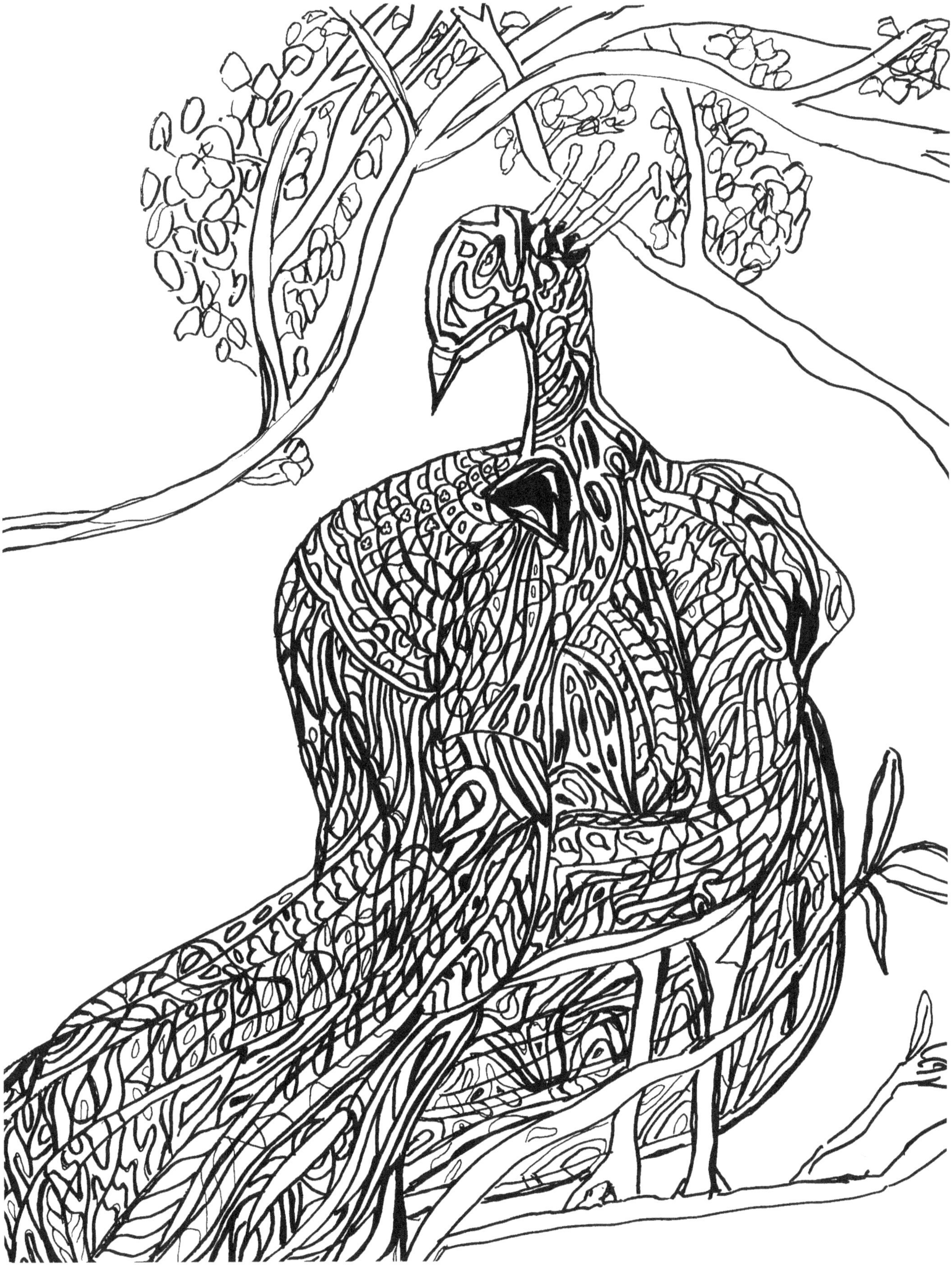

Cut Here

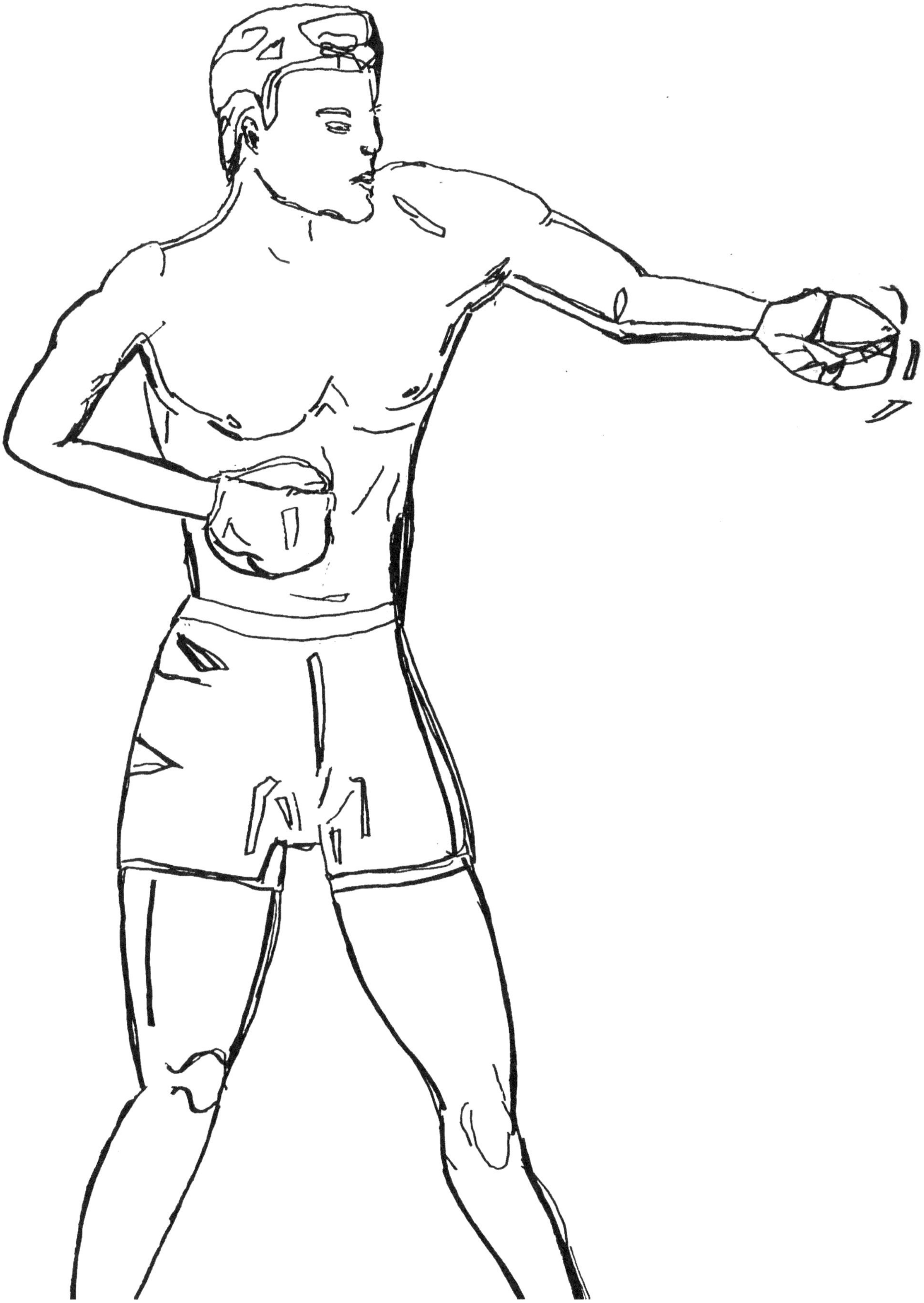

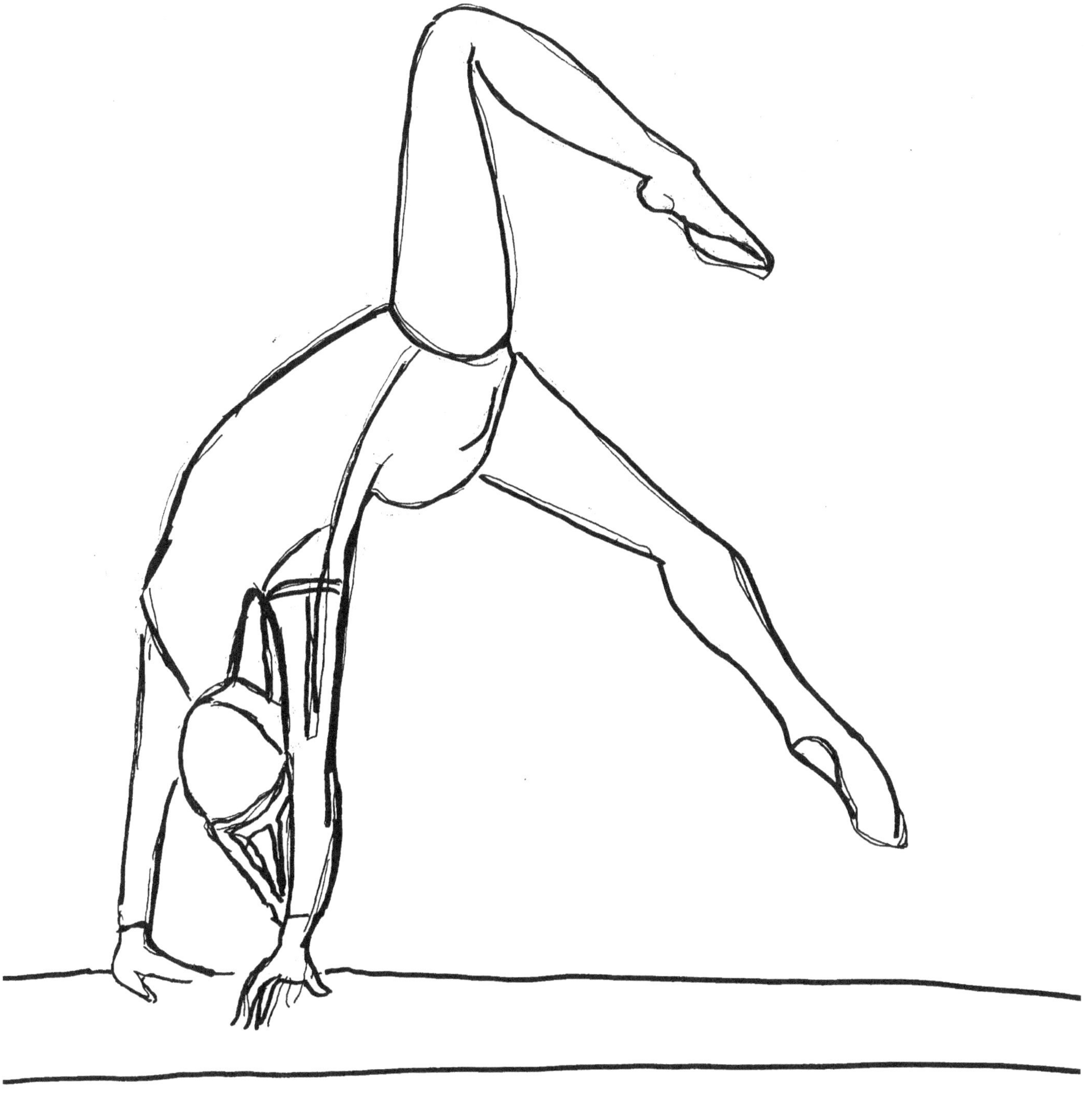

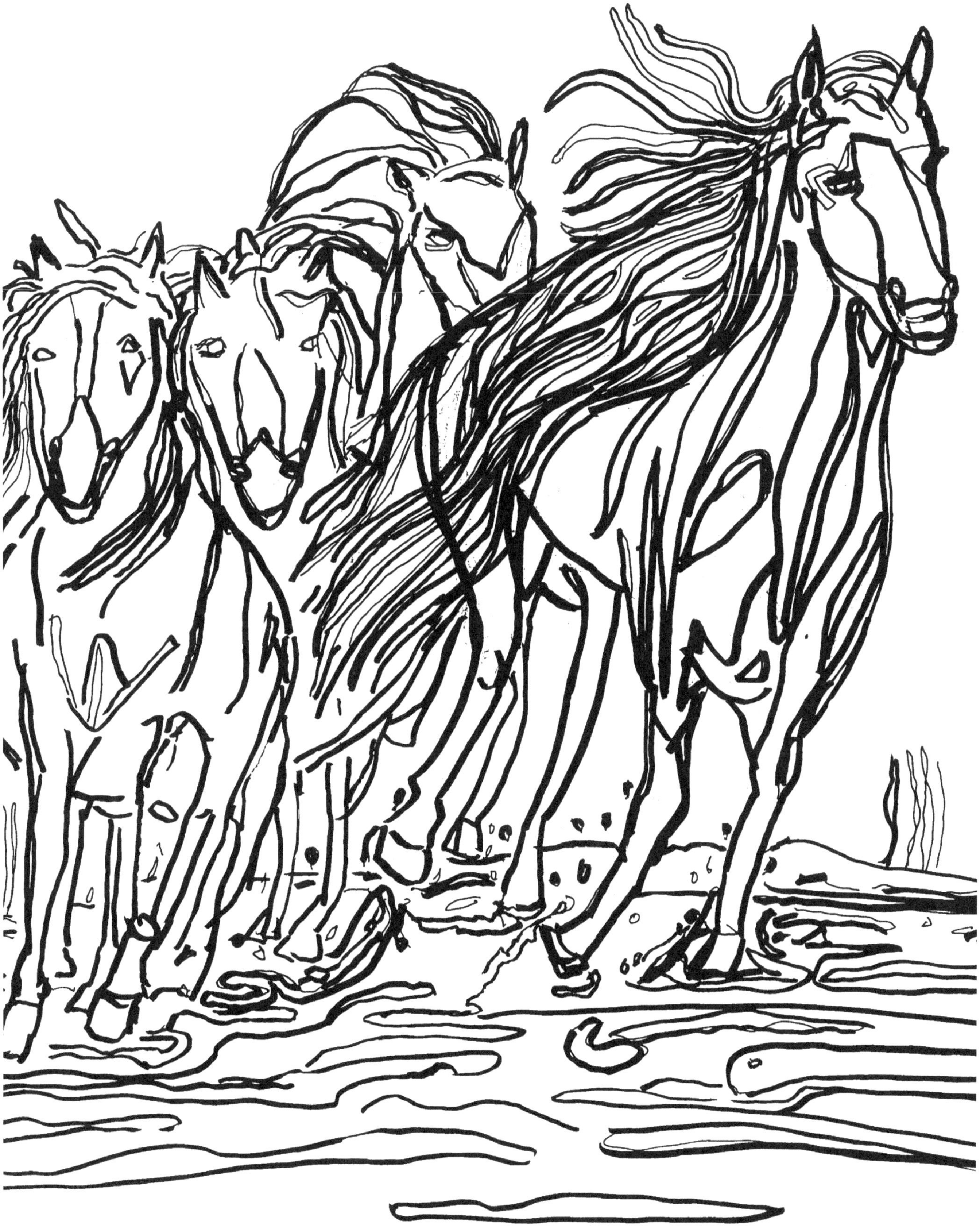

Cut Here

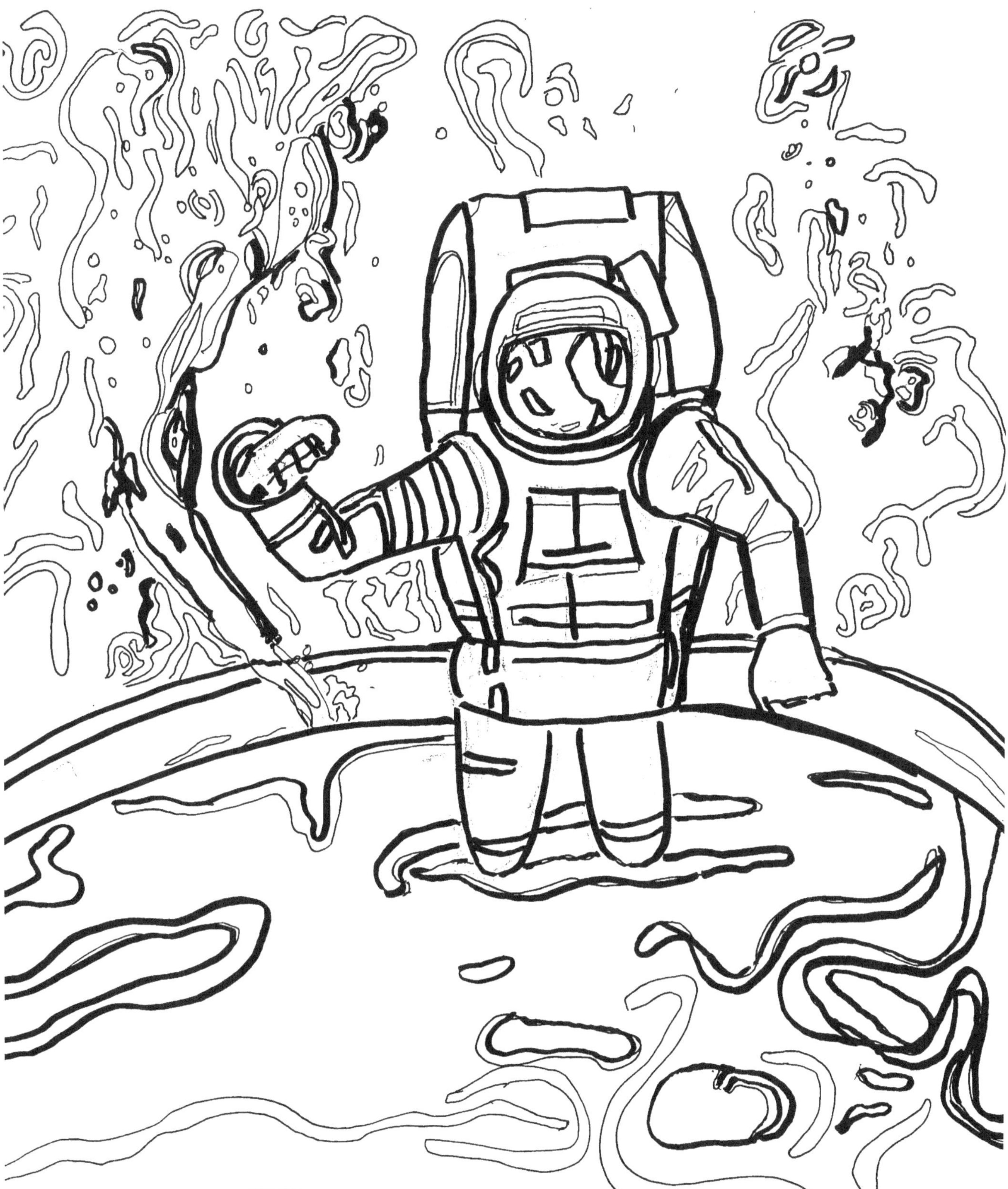

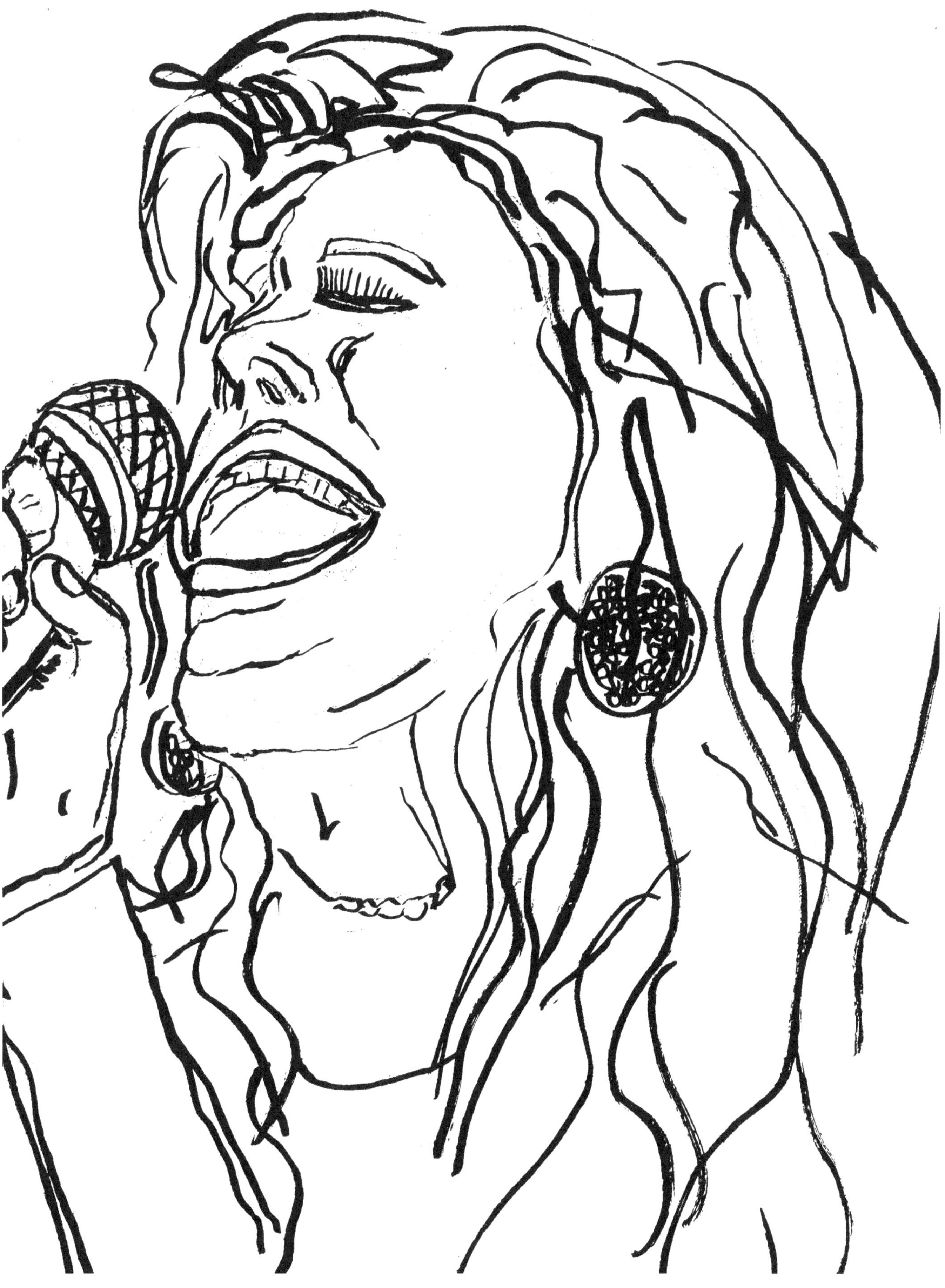

Cut Here

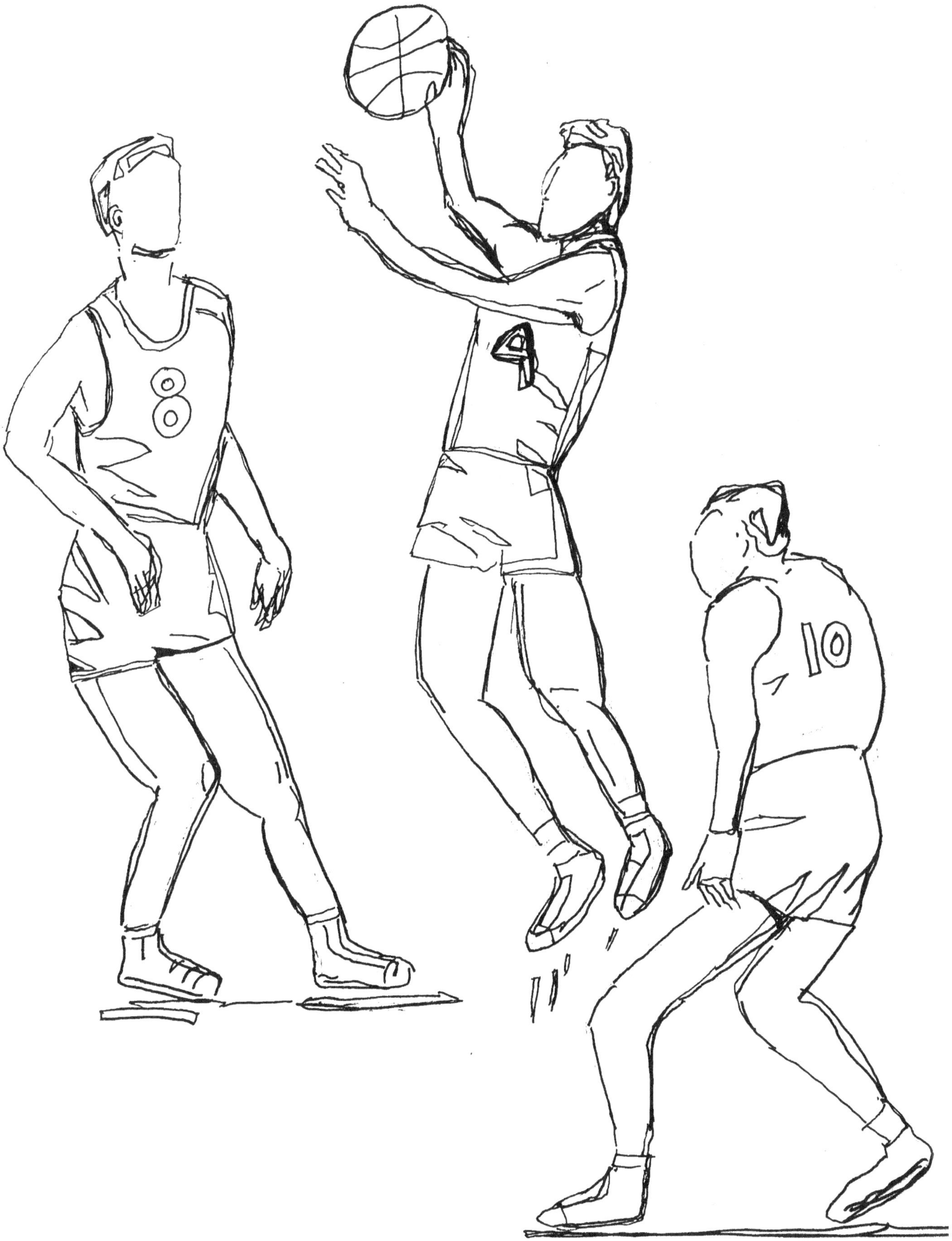

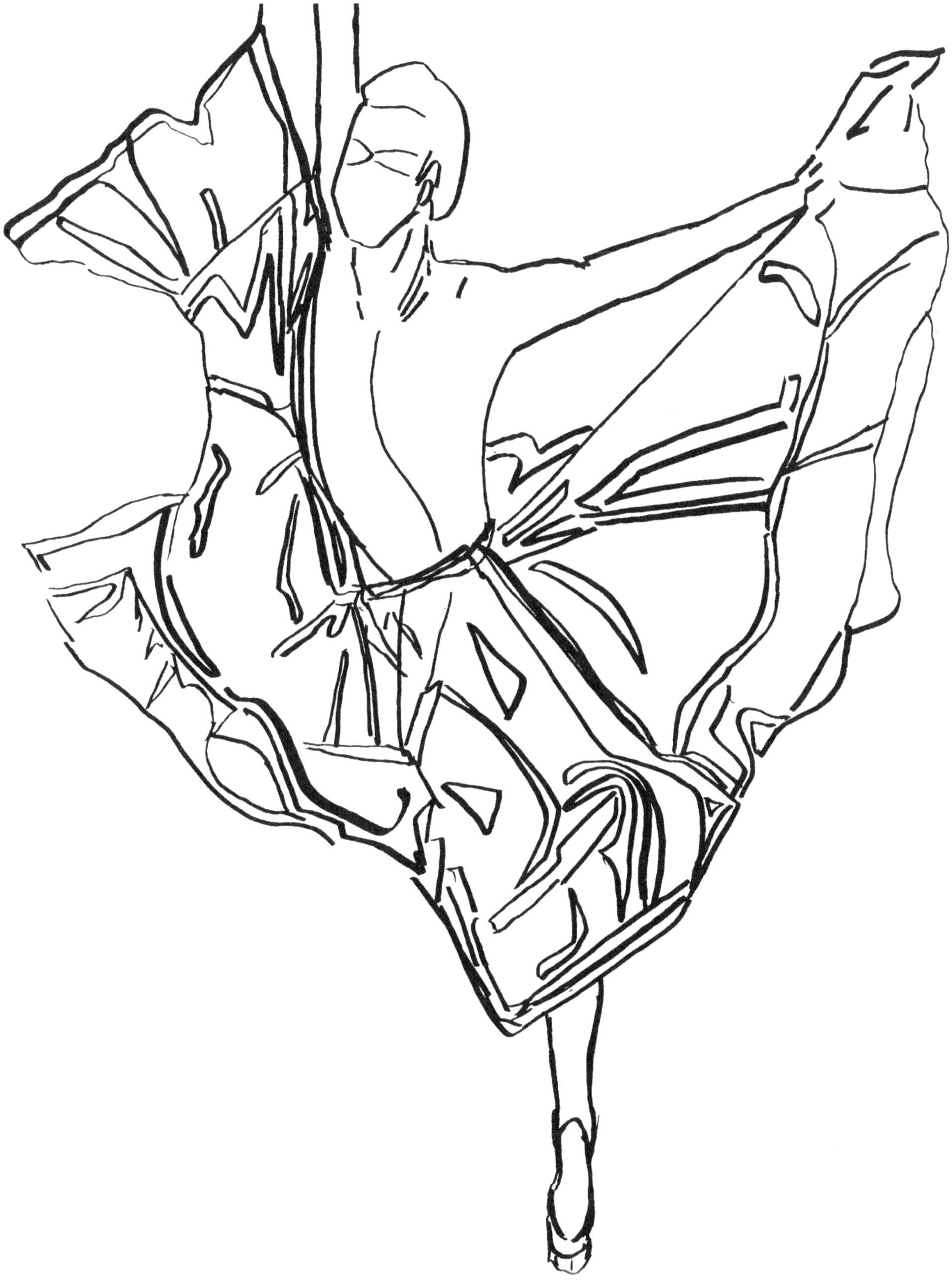

Cut Here

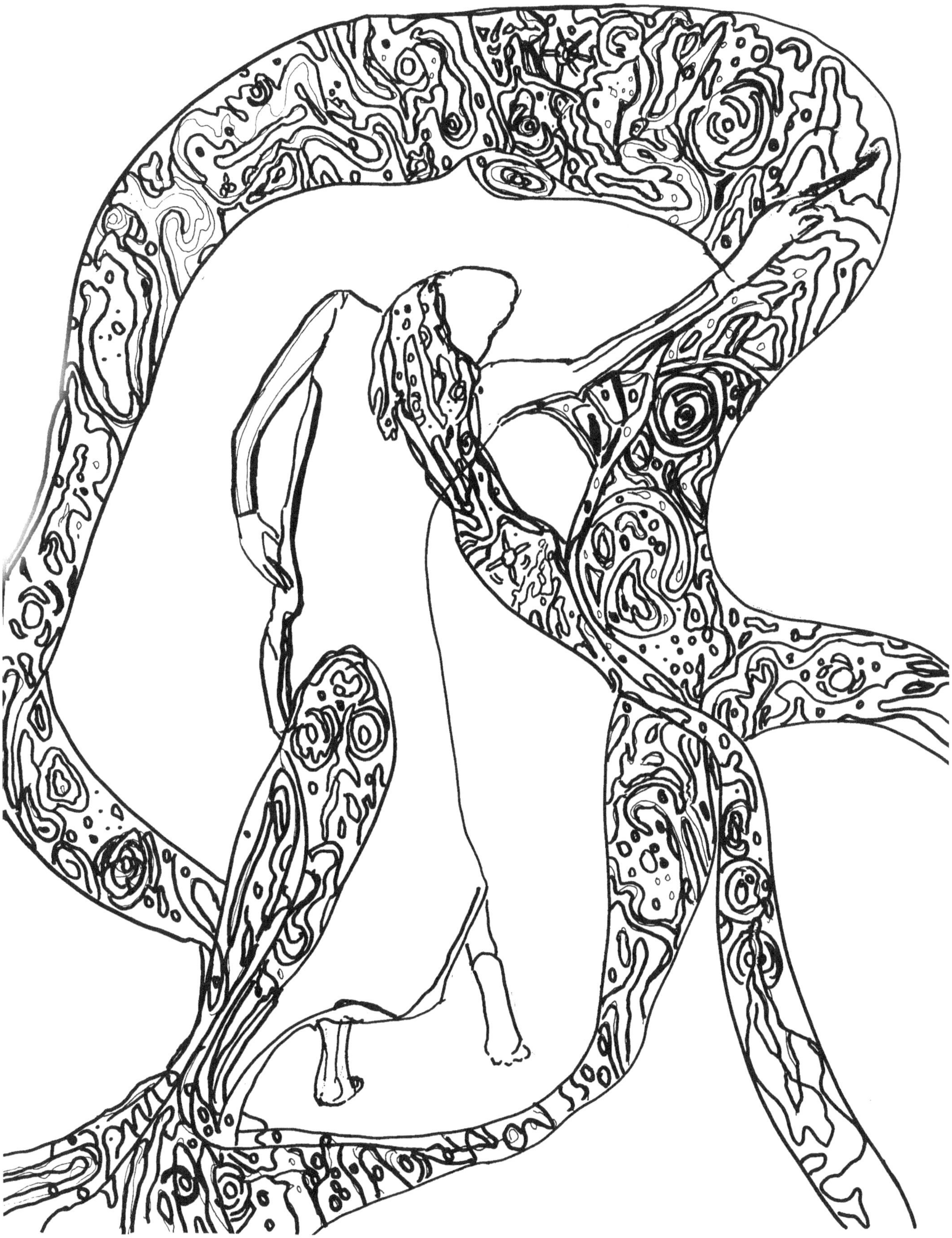

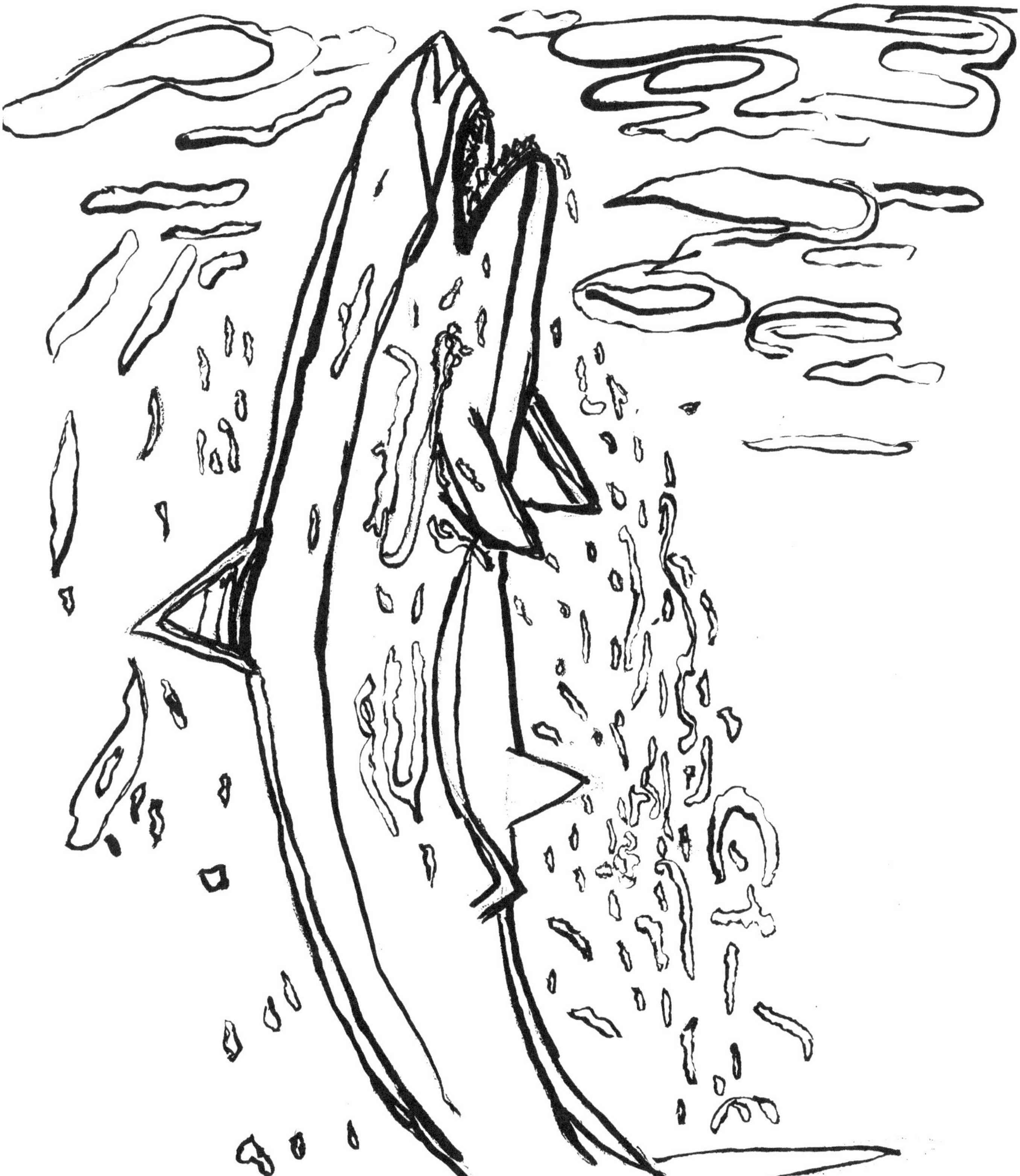

Cut Here

www.ingramcontent.com/pod-product-compliance
Lightning Source LLC
Chambersburg PA
CBHW080859220526
45467CB00008B/2568
* 9 7 9 8 7 2 3 8 2 8 0 2 5 *